fashion
HACKS

USE SIMPLE SEWING TECHNIQUES TO RECYCLE, REUSE, AND REVAMP YOUR CLOTHES FOR A MORE MINDFUL APPROACH TO FASHION

janine chisholm sullivan

CICO BOOKS
LONDON NEW YORK

For my mum who I miss greatly, for my dad who is the bravest person I know, and for my guiding lights, my sisters Shellee and Kirstie. I love you all to bits. x

This edition published in 2021 by CICO Books
An imprint of Ryland Peters & Small
20–21 Jockey's Fields, London
WC1R 4BW
341 E 116th St, New York, NY 10012

www.rylandpeters.com

First published in 2012 as *Thrifty Style*

10 9 8 7 6 5 4 3 2 1

Text © Janine Chisholm Sullivan 2012
Design, photography, and illustration ©
CICO Books 2012

A CIP catalog record for this book is available from the Library of Congress and the British Library.

ISBN: 978-1-78249-927-5

Printed in China

Editor: Sarah Hoggett
Photography: Chris Bracewell, Emma Mitchell, and Martin Norris
Styling: Rob Merrett, Jemima Bradley
Designer and art director: Valentina
Illustrator: Stephen Dew

Contents

Introduction

We all have clothes in our wardrobes that we don't wear, either because they don't really suit or fit us any more or because they're a bit dated or out of style. Or perhaps, for example, you found a wonderful vintage dress in a thrift store or garage sale, but never knew quite what to do with it. *Fashion Hacks* will show you how to transform these clothes into unique, one-off pieces that reflect your personality and lifestyle—and without breaking the bank!

Customizing, reworking, and redesigning all amount to the same thing, which is to reuse old (and new) clothes, breathing life into them. You might want to copy a current look that you have seen in a magazine, recreate a certain style from a music video, or put together a combination of different looks. *Fashion Hacks* will show you how to mix it up, whether you want to dress up, dress down, or simply add your own personal stamp on an item.

All you have to know is... THERE ARE NO RULES! Mix the old with new, the elegant with punk; the combinations are endless, limited only by your imagination!

Fashion Hacks will also show you how to get as much mileage out of one piece of clothing as possible. Check out the polka dot dress on page 62, for example: I manage to create three items from this 1980s polyester dress with only a scrap of fabric left over at the end. See the Folklore Dress on page 86, where I put two items together to make one fabulous look.

So the clothes you want to customize and adapt may not be exactly like the ones in this book? The techniques and ideas are easily transferable. Even if you haven't done much sewing before or feel your skills are a bit rusty, don't panic: on pages 109–126 you'll find a handy reference section on sewing techniques. A few simple sewing skills will open up a wealth of possibility.

Sustainability is key here. I'm passionate about recycling and *Fashion Hacks* is also about absorbing clothes back into the environment when they've reached the end of their use. As a personal shopper and stylist, I buy a lot of clothes and often come across beautiful items that have absolutely nothing wrong with them except, perhaps, a broken zipper. Once you know how to replace the zipper, adapt the piece to suit your style and body shape, and add a few finishing touches of your own, you'll have what amounts to a brand-new garment—far better than something ending up in landfill.

I hope that *Fashion Hacks* will help, inspire, and support you in what you wish to create. Good luck— and the best advice I can give you is to have fun!

Janine Chisholm Sullivan

Chapter 1
Embellishing

Embellishment means changing the surface of the item of clothing, as opposed to the outline of the garment, and can encompass everything from simple embroidery, adding trims such as ribbon or crochet, stitching on sparkly beads or pretty buttons, applying decorative binding around a neckline or armholes, distressing the fabric, and much more. Remember, too, that decoration doesn't have to be particularly "feminine"—it could mean adding an exposed metal zipper to your favorite blouse or leaving a raw edge on a silk dress for a cool, contemporary urban edge. Whatever embellishments you choose, you can totally update and change the look of the original piece with very little effort.

Blinding binding dress

Bindings can add an individual stamp to any item of clothing—so let yourself go on necklines and armholes galore!

STEP 3

Fold in

Top stitch on the right side of the strap

STEP 5

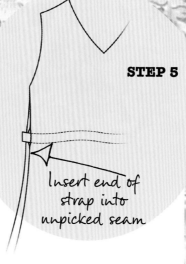

Insert end of strap into unpicked seam

Binding comes in so many wonderful colors and designs— hearts, polka dots, you name it. You can also make your own (see page 119).

I chose this dress as I liked the hotchpotch feel of it. In its original condition, it looked like a housedress. The vintage print binding made it into more of a day dress.

YOU WILL NEED
• Floral dress
• Bias binding, ⅝ in. (1.5 cm) wide
• Dress or top with adjustable straps to use for the belt
• Matching thread

Take ⅝-in. (1.5-cm) seam allowances throughout, unless otherwise stated.

CUTTING THE BINDING
• I used three different patterned bindings for this dress, but you can bind the neckline and

armholes in the same fabric if you prefer—or even use a ready-made binding.
• Measure the armholes and cut two lengths of fabric on the bias to this length plus 1 in. (2.5 cm) extra on each for overlap.
• Measure the neckline and cut one length of fabric on the bias to this length plus 2 in. (5 cm) extra for overlap.

1 Cut pieces of fabric to the required length and no more than 1 in. (2.5 cm) wide for the armhole and neckline bindings. Bind the armholes and neckline, following the instructions on page 119.

2 Remove the adjustable straps of the dress or top that you're using for the belt.

3 To make a tab for the end of the belt, cut two strips of fabric twice the width of the strap plus a little excess for folding in. (I cut

small pieces of fabric from the hem of the dress, but you could use some of the binding fabric if you prefer.) Center the non-adjustable end of each strap on a tab, right side down. Fold over the sides of the tab, press in place, and topstitch all around on the right side for a funky look.

4 Turn the dress wrong side out. Decide where you want to position the belt; I decided to place it below the bustline, about 4½ in. (11.5 cm) down from the top of the side seam. Unpick about 1 in. (2.5 cm) of each side seam of the dress at this point.

5 Insert the adjustable end of each strap into an unpicked section side seam and baste (tack) in place. Stitch the side seams back together, securing the waist straps in place.

6 Turn the dress right side out, press, and go!

STYLIST'S TIP

Sewing ribbons or straps into the waistlines of tops and dresses is the perfect way to give your item a more tailored look. You can insert the straps or ribbon into the waistline wherever you want: they can be level with the waist or just below the bustline for an empire-line shape.

Level

1 # Sleeveless thermal top

Thermals do need not be hidden under clothing—they can look good, as well as keeping you warm. Follow this project and show off your designer piece to your friends!

STEP 2

Stretch straps as you stitch on the lace

STEP 3

Unpick side seam and insert end of lace

STEP 4

Restitch the unpicked side seam

The key to customizing a top, or any piece of clothing, is to stick with the essence of it. Why did you buy it? Was it for the color or the texture? Do you want to highlight a certain part of it—for example, showing the straps under an open-necked top?

The vintage buttons that I used here were found in an old sewing machine that I bought recently from a thrift store. The best finds tend to happen like this—by accident—and it is always nice if there is a story behind them, as this makes the final piece even more special.

YOU WILL NEED
- **Sleeveless thermal top**
- **Coordinating vintage lace and ribbon preferably with a bit of stretch (amount depends on the size of the top)**
- **7 vintage buttons (optional)**

1 **Measure the straps of the top.** Cut two lengths of vintage lace, each 6 in. (15 cm) longer than the straps.

2 **Pin the lace in place on the straps,** folding it under at each end for a neat finish. Zigag stitch the lace in place, using a stitch just slightly narrower than the strap and stretching the straps of the top as you go, so that they remain elasticated. If you wish, hand stitch a button to one or both ends of each strap.

3 **At the front of the top, measure under the bust line** from side seam to side seam, add 10 in. (25 cm) to this measurement to ensure that you have enough to cover the stretch, and cut a piece of lace to this length. Under the bustline, unpick a short section of the side seam just wider than the lace. Starting from the center front and working outward—first

toward the left side seam and then toward the right—using a narrow zigzag stitch and stretching the top slightly as you go, machine stitch the lace in place. Tuck the ends of the lace into the unpicked sections of side seam and cut off any excess.

4 **Turn the top inside out.** Pin the unpicked sections of side seam back together. Set your zigzag stitch length to the width of the existing seam and machine stitch the unpicked sections of side seam.

SEWING TIP
Match the color of your threads to the materials—here I used black thread as a top thread and a lighter color in the bobbin when attaching the lace to the straps.

1970s folk top

This 1970s smock top was perfect for dyeing, as it was 100 percent cotton and would therefore take the dye well, while the embroidery would dye to a darker color to show off the design to maximum effect.

STEP 3

Add beads for the flower centers

Stitch around embroidered flowers

Ideally, you must use a blouse that is cotton or mainly cotton, as a synthetic one will not take the dye, unless you use a specialized one suitable for synthetic fabrics. Be mindful that the thread could be polyester, which would mean that you have an evenly dyed top but the stitching would be in its original color—not necessarily a good look!

I decided to cover the existing ribbon which sat just above the hemline, as I felt it needed to be modernized. I stitched new ribbon over the old one and also across the raglan line of the sleeves, which broke up the contrast between the dark and the light that the dyeing process had produced.

YOU WILL NEED
• Cotton smock top
• Fabric dye
• Salt
• 3 yd (3 m) ribbon, ⅝ in. (1.5 cm) wide
• Embellishments of your choice—beads, gems, various threads
• Coordinating threads
• Needle and thread or beading needle and thread

1 Rinse your top in warm water so that all of it is wet; this will ensure that the color spreads evenly. Dye your top, following the dye manufacturer's instructions. (See also page 126.) Allow to dry.

2 If a trim goes over the side seams of the garment, unpick a section of the seam at the relevant point. Insert the end of your new trim into the unpicked section and pin in place. Machine stitch along each side of the trim, as close to the edge as possible.

STEP 2

Pin ribbon, then machine stitch onto top

3 Now for the freestitching: you can use any stitch and any color of thread you want! I stitched around the embroidered flowers and then used large beads as the flower heads and pearl beads at the ends of some of the branches, to make it look as if the sun was catching them.

SEWING TIPS
• I used ordinary sewing thread in a color to match the beads, but you could use a beading thread if you prefer. Beads can also add a little weight to the item.
• You can transfer images by drawing them on greaseproof paper with a wax crayon, turning the paper over, and ironing the design onto the fabric.

Day dress with crochet trim

Applying textiles to items of clothing can make such a difference and isn't necessarily difficult to do—the secret lies in the preparation.

For this project, you can use an existing piece of crochet or crochet a decorative panel yourself.

YOU WILL NEED
- **Dress** (this one is raw silk)
- **Approx. 2 yd (2 m) coordinating ribbon for the straps** (check measurement of existing straps), ⅝ in. (1.5 cm) wide
- **Matching thread**
- **2 crocheted doilies or pieces of crocheted fabric**
- **Buttons for the end of the straps** (optional)

Take ⅜-in. (1-cm) seam allowances throughout, unless otherwise stated.

1 Try the dress on first to check that you are happy with the length of the straps as they are. Turn the dress wrong side out. Remove the straps carefully at the stitching points; if there is a facing, unpick a section as the new straps will have to go under the facing. Place pins at the points where the straps meet the dress as a guide for when you attach the new straps.

2 Measure the length of one strap, add 1¼ in. (3 cm), and cut two lengths of ribbon to this measurement. Using tailor's chalk, mark on the ribbons where the stitching was on the original straps. Pin the new ribbon straps on the dress, with the right side of the ribbon (if there is one) facing upward. Baste (tack) in place, sliding the ribbons under the facing if there is one.

3 Turn the dress right side out and put it back on to check that you are happy with the strap length; wiggle your shoulders to check that the straps don't slide off. If necessary, get a friend to re-pin the ribbon straps to the correct length.

4 Take the dress off. Straight stitch the ribbon straps in place using a medium-length stitch. Re-stitch the facing back in place if necessary.

5 If you wish, hand sew buttons onto the dress where the straps meet the dress. As well as being decorative, this covers up any wobbly stitching that you may not want anyone else to see!

6 Lay the dress flat, right side out, with the front facing up. Center the crocheted fabric or doily on top of the dress and pin in place. Measure from the ends of the crocheted piece to the side seams to make sure that you have positioned it centrally. Baste (tack) the crocheted piece onto the dress.

7 Hold the dress up to check that you are happy with the positioning and that the crocheted piece is completely flat. Once you are satisfied, machine zigzag stitch as close to the edge of the crocheted piece as possible, stitching on the right side of the dress. Straight stitch another line parallel to the first, ¼ in. (6 mm) inside this stitching line.

8 Lay the dress flat, with the back facing up. Center the second crocheted piece on top and pin, then baste (tack) in place. Stitch in place, as in step 7.

9 Turn the dress wrong side out. Cut away the back of the dress from under the crochet, being careful not to cut through the stitching that holds the crochet in place.

STEP 5

Sew on buttons

STEP 6

Pin, then baste the crochet in place

STEP 9

Cut away the back of the dress fabric under the crochet

SEWING TIPS

• Keep the dress and crocheted piece flat on the table with one hand while basting (tacking), so that the crocheted piece does not slip out of place.

• When stitching the crochet to the dress, feed the dress into the machine carefully, keeping both hands flat, so that the fabric does not pucker and the crochet lies flat.

DESIGNER TIP If your crocheted piece features a specific motif, such as a flower, snip around the edge of the shape to cut out the section that you want to use.

Silk jewelry top

There is a huge range of beads available to buy, but all that choice could lead to an empty bank balance—so why not bring an old top back to life by using costume jewelry from your local thrift store? For the hemline, I used a necklace made out of wooden beads painted with a tribal influence. Around the neckline I placed a string of multicolored plastic beads.

You can revamp any item of clothing using this method—a dress, blouse, or other type of top—but do not use anything that is made of jersey fabric, as the beads will break. And bear in mind the weight of the beads and how much stretch or tension the fabric underneath is going to be under when the garment is worn, as this will determine how much stitching you will need to attach the jewelry.

YOU WILL NEED
• A suitable item of clothing
• Matching jewelry—for example, a broken necklace
• Ordinary sewing thread or beading thread
• Wire cutters or pliers (depending on the type of stringing material used in the necklaces)

1 Lay the top front up on your work surface, or place it on a mannequin (see page 111 for how to make your own mannequin bodice) and place your necklace in position. I doubled up my string of multi-colored plastic beads and attached it to the neckline. Using sewing or beading thread and a regular hand sewing needle, oversew between the beads. The intervals at which you need to sew depend on the weight of the beads and how they hang when you hold the top up; I made my stitches at roughly 1-in. (2.5-cm) intervals.

2 I then attached a necklace of wooden beads to the hemline in the same way, to add a bit of weight to the top. I also cut off the sparkly loop clasp at the end—

partly because the necklace was too long for the hem of the top, but also because I wanted to use the loop as a focal point at the neckline—and reattached it by tying thread through the loop and around one string of the neckline necklace, tying both ends in a firm double knot.

SEWING TIPS
• If you use plastic beading thread, make sure you tie it in a double knot at the end, as it can come undone very easily.
• Alternatively, use regular sewing thread in a color that matches the top, so that the thread disappears into the background.

STEP 2

Oversew the stringing material between the beads

Tweed riding jacket

This is a wardrobe staple: you can wear it with jeans and a T-shirt or team it with your smart office dress. I used worn leather from an old coat for the elbow patches, but you can use sew-on patches (which come in a wide range of colors and have holes to sew through) if you prefer.

YOU WILL NEED
- Lady's wool or wool mix tweed jacket—preferably with a free-hanging lining
- Soft, lightweight leather or suede off-cuts for elbow patches, collar, and pocket detail
- Latex-based adhesive and spatula (you could even use a stirrer from a coffee shop!)
- Buttons (you may want to buy an extra one to sew inside the jacket lining as a spare)
- Buttonhole thread
- Dressmaker's carbon paper and tracing wheel
- Bag or a belt with a leather or leather-effect shoulder strap for back waist detail
- Machine thread and specialist topstitching thread to match the tweed and leather
- Leather machine needles

Take ⅝-in. (1.5-cm) seam allowances throughout, unless otherwise stated.

1 Put the jacket on and ask a friend to pin where you want the top and bottom of the elbow patches to be sewn and then decide on the width. Make a template out of paper, cut it out, and pin onto the jacket to check the positioning and size. Once you're happy with everything, draw around the templates on the wrong side of the leather, adding a ⅜-in. (1-cm) seam allowance all around, and cut out.

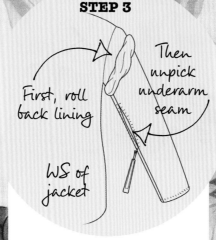

STEP 3

First, roll back lining

Then unpick underarm seam

WS of jacket

2 Snip V-shaped notches into the seam allowance of the patches all the way around to remove bulk. Spread latex-based adhesive over the seam allowance on the back of the leather patches, leave until slightly tacky to the touch, then fold over the seam allowance all around and press down gently with your fingers. Leave overnight.

PRACTICAL TIPS
- Before you apply the adhesive, have a practice attempt at folding over the edges of the leather patch to make sure that you have snipped far enough into them.
- To prevent glue from blocking your machine, spray silicone spray on your machine needle and machine bed.

3 Turn the jacket inside out and pull the sleeves through. Unpick the sleeve linings at the cuffs, and roll the linings back so that they're out of the way. Unpick the tweed sleeve underarm seams to

the length of the patches plus about 1 in. (2.5 cm) either side.

4 Set your sewing machine to the longest stitch length, but do not thread it. Slowly stitch around each leather elbow patch, close to the edge; this will create a series of holes for you to sew through.

5 Turn the tweed sleeves right side out and mark where the leather patches will go with tailor's chalk. Using a matching or contrasting colour of topstitching thread, either hand stitch (using running stitch) or machine stitch (using a leather needle) the patches in place. Turn the tweed sleeves wrong side out again. Machine stitch the underarm sleeve seams back in place.

6 Pull the sleeve linings back down, pin, and slipstitch the cuffs in place.

7 Remove the old buttons. Using buttonhole thread, attach the new ones.

SEWING TIP
Make sure that the new buttons fit through the existing buttonholes. If the holes aren't quite large enough, snip into them and oversew the raw edge with buttonhole thread to prevent fraying.

Tailors' tacks

STEP 8
Unpick upper collar

STEP 11
Topstitch leather collar to jacket

8 Now replace the existing upper collar with a new leather one! Work three pairs of tailor's tacks along the neckline edge of the upper collar and the neckline edge of the jacket as balance marks for later. Unpick the tweed upper collar. Lay it flat, wrong side up, and press flat.

9 Place the right side of the tweed upper collar on the wrong side of the leather, with dressmaker's carbon paper right side down in between. Holding the collar flat, trace around the outer edge and over the existing stitching lines with a tracing wheel, then transfer the balance marks to the leather. Add a seam allowance of ⅜–⅝ in. (1–1.5 cm) all around and cut out.

10 Snip V-shaped notches into the seam allowance all the way around the leather collar to allow for folding over neatly. Using a spatula, spread latex-based adhesive evenly over the wrong side of the seam allowance of the leather, leave until touch dry, then fold over the seam allowance to the wrong side. Cut off the corners to remove any unnecessary bulk.

11 Using a leather needle and matching the balance marks, topstitch the leather collar to the jacket along the three inner

edges. Using a contrasting thread, work another line of topstitching around the three outer edges of the leather collar, stitching as close to the collar edge as possible.

DESIGNER TIP
Why not remove the entire collar and use this as a template to create an upper/under collar constructed out of leather? Or alternatively another fabric as an under collar?

12 Now for the back belt detail. Put the jacket on and ask a friend to pin where your waist sits on the back of the jacket. Measure the width of the bag shoulder strap that you are using and add 1 in. (2.5 cm). Unpick the two back darts by this amount at the waist.

13 On the unpicked dart section, mark the top and bottom of the belt with a pin. Lay the jacket down, measure from the center

back seam to the back dart, add ⅜ in. (1 cm), and cut each end of the bag strap to this length. The metal rings that hold the strap in place on the bag need to overlap each other slightly at the center back so that both rings can be secured into place.

14 Turn the jacket inside out and lift the lining up, so that you don't accidentally stitch it to the belt. Insert the cut ends of the bag strap into the unpicked sections of seam. Using a leather machine needle, stitch the straps in place. Zigzag stitch the raw edges of the straps, too, if your machine is able to, as the straps may add a little strain to the seam. Finish off the seams.

15 Turn the jacket right side out and lay it flat. Using buttonhole thread, hand stitch the rings of the strap to the jacket at the

STEP 14
Lift up lining

Insert belt or bag straps through unpicked seams

STEP 12
Dart

Side seam

Waistline

WS of jacket

Unpick width of bag shoulder strap plus 1 in

STEP 16a

Cut leather strip

Remove pocket flap

STEP 16b

Restitch the pocket flap

center back seam, overlapping them slightly. Pull the jacket lining back down.

16 Cut a strip of leather ⅝ in. (1.5 cm) deep by the width of the pocket. Unpick the flap above the top right-hand pocket and topstitch the raw edges of the leather onto the top edge of the pocket. Restitch the pocket flap above this leather strip along the original stitching line.

Shoulder sparkle top

Never waste left-over fabric! This old polo-neck sweater has been embellished with sequined panels, which are the off-cuts from the sparkly 1920s-style dress (see page 44).

Place sparkly fabric panels on sweater

Mark width and depth of panel on sweater

STEP 1

YOU WILL NEED
• Sparkly fabric (which could be left over from another project)
• Woolen/jersey polo-neck sweater
• Pack of ballpoint needles
• Matching and contrasting sewing threads

Take ⅝-in. (1.5-cm) seam allowances throughout unless otherwise stated.

1 **Lay the polo-neck sweater on your work surface** with the front facing up toward you, or place it on a mannequin (see page 111 for how to make your own mannequin bodice). Place the sparkly fabric right side up on one shoulder, aligning it with the shoulder line seam and the armhole line, to see how it looks and check that you have enough fabric. Measure how wide and how deep you want the embellishment to be and mark this shape on the polo-neck sweater with tailor's chalk.

DESIGNER TIP
My remnant of sparkly fabric had one heavily beaded edge, which indicated the original neckline. I positioned this beaded edge along the armhole line to create a nice, decorative edge.

2 **Transfer this shape to tracing paper** and add a ⅛-in. (3-mm) seam allowance to each side, except for the heavily beaded edge. Cut out the tracing-paper shape to use as a pattern.

3 **Place the pattern on the wrong side of the sparkly fabric,** draw around it, and cut out. Turn the pattern over and repeat, so that you have one left and one right shoulder embellishment.

4 **Using small, sharp scissors,** remove ⅛ in. (3 mm) of sequins from each edge except for the heavily sequinned edge. Following the chalked line on the wrong side of the fabric, fold these edges under, pin, and baste (tack) in place.

5 **Using a contrasting thread,** baste (tack) the sequined pieces onto the sweater.

SEWING TIP
If any sequins or beads are loose, stitch them in place by hand, being sure to tie a knot in your thread first.

6 **Set your machine to a narrow zigzag stitch** and use a ballpoint needle. Starting at one end of the shoulder seam and reverse stitching at the start and finish, stitch the embellishment on around the three sides where you removed the sequins. Remove the basting (tacking) stitches.

7 **Using matching sewing thread,** slipstitch the heavily beaded edge in place for a neat finish.

Why not combine a high-street silk top with a decorative table decoration and get to practice your shirring skills at the same time? This top will fit any occasion!

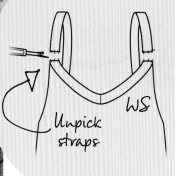

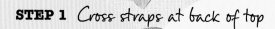

STEP 1 *Cross straps at back of top*

Unpick straps WS

Stitch cross shape to hold straps in place WS

Here, I have used a 1950s matt linen doily, which works really well against the shiny silkiness of the top. You will need a piece of table linen that is big enough to fit from the top of the center front neckline of the silk top to the top of the bodice line on the center back. The original top was quite baggy, so I added shirring to the back of it to pull it in slightly and give it more shape.

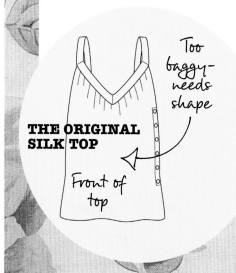

Too baggy— needs shape

THE ORIGINAL SILK TOP

Front of top

YOU WILL NEED
- Silk top with straps
- At least 3 yd (3 m) elastic thread
- Doily or other piece of decorative table linen
- 4-in. (10-cm) metal zipper

SEWING TIP
You will need to use a tailor's dummy for this project.

1 Turn the top wrong side out. Using a seam ripper, carefully unpick the straps from the back of the top. Cross the back straps over each other, then reattach them in their original place. Where the straps cross over one another, stitch a cross shape within a stitched square to secure them in place.

2 Turn the top right side out. Using tailor's chalk, mark on the back of the top where you want the shirring to begin. Mark a point 3 in. (7.5 cm) down from the center back and then mark 2 in. (5 cm) either side of this point. Mark three more rows below this line, ¼ in. (6 mm) apart.

3 Wind elastic thread manually onto the bobbin of your machine. Using regular thread as the top thread, zigzag stitch along each line in turn. Pull the thread ends through to the wrong side and knot the thread and elastic securely together.

SEWING TIPS
- Practice shirring on a spare piece of silk fabric first, to make sure you get the stitch length right.
- Stretch the fabric out flat when you stitch the second and subsequent rows of shirring.

STEP 4

Pin doily to top

STEP 5 +

Mark
and cut
neckline

STEP 7

Adjust doily to fit shoulders

4 Put the silk top on a tailor's dummy, with the front facing toward you. Decide where you want the center front of the neckline to be and make two marks on both the top and the doily—the first one at your desired neckline and the second one 2 in. (5 cm) down from this point. (This allows plenty of room for an overlap between the top and the doily.) Pin the doily to the top at the lower of the two marks on the neckline and at the sides. Repeat on the back of the top.

5 Remove the doily and place it right side up on your work surface. Working from the top marks on the front and back and adding a ⅜-in. (1-cm) seam allowance, mark a circular (or rectangular) neckline in the center of the doily. Cut along the marked line.

6 Put the top back on the dummy, with the front facing you. Aligning the doily with the lower of the two marks that you made in step 4, pin and baste (tack) the doily to the top. Repair any broken parts with buttonhole thread if necessary.

7 It is unlikely that the doily will fit the shoulders of the top perfectly, so you will need to make some adjustments. With the top still on the dummy, pin the doily across the shoulders, making sure that it sits flat. Cut away any excess doily ⅜ in. (1 cm) above the pins on each side.

8 Take the top off the dummy, fold under ⅜ in. (1 cm) of the doily on each side of the shoulder seams, and stitch in place. Press flat.

9 Turn the top inside out and remove the front straps completely. Turn under and machine stitch the raw edge of the neckline.

10 The circular opening will not be big enough to fit your head through, so you also need to insert a zipper. Place the zipper right side down on the wrong side of one shoulder, with the zipper pull at the neckline. Baste (tack) the zipper to the shoulder seams. Stitch the zipper in place, then turn the top right side out and cut away a small section of the doily along the shoulder so that you can open the zipper, taking care not to cut through any of the stitches that hold the zipper in place.

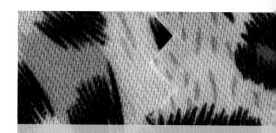

Out of Africa jumpsuit

Jumpsuits can provide a cool, no-nonsense alternative to separates or a summer dress—an instant hot look with just one item!

This jumpsuit needed to jump out of the '80s and into the present day for a timeless, romantic safari look.

The amount of cord that you will need for the beltline depends on your own waist measurement and on how tight or loose you want the waistline to be. In the materials list below, I've erred on the generous side!

YOU WILL NEED
• Jumpsuit (preferably 100 percent cotton, although linen would also be suitable)
• Fabric dye
• Household or dyeing salt
• Up to 1⅝ yd (1.5 m) rope cord, ¼ in. (6 mm) thick, for belt
• Up to 2¼ yd (2 m) rope cord, ⅛ in. (2.5 mm) thick, for ankle/shoulder ties
• Clear adhesive tape for the ends of the cord ties
• Eyelet kit and hammer
• 8–12 large eyelets
• Buttons (optional)
• Large toggle for belt and four smaller toggles for the shoulders and pants legs
• Old jewelry

Take ⅝-in. (1.5-cm) seam allowances throughout, unless otherwise stated.

1 Rinse the jumpsuit in warm water so that all of it is damp; this will ensure that the color spreads evenly. Dye the jumpsuit, following the dye manufacturer's instructions. (See also page 126.) Wash separately, then allow to dry naturally.

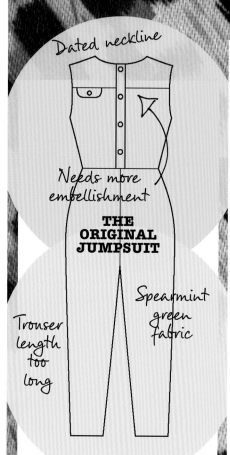

Dated neckline

Needs more embellishment

THE ORIGINAL JUMPSUIT

Trouser length too long

Spearmint green fabric

2 Put the jumpsuit on in front of a full-length mirror and decide what kind of hemline you want. Think about which shoes you will be wearing with the jumpsuit and try them on with it. And bear in mind that a belt may raise the overall hemline. I opted for a fresh, utility look, with eyelets in the hems and at the waistline, through which I threaded cord ties. Pin the legs at the length you want. Measure, mark with tailor's chalk, and cut the legs to the required length, remembering

to allow for the hem; the eyelets that I used on the legs were ⅝ in. (1.5 cm) in diameter, so I made the hem 1¼ in. (3 cm) deep. Keep the cut-off fabric, as you will need it later. Hem the legs of the jumpsuit (see page 109).

3 Remove the existing buttons and change them to fit the look you are aiming for.

4 You are now going to make adjustable tie shoulder straps. Open up the seams of the pieces of fabric that you cut off the hem in step 2 and press. Following the cross grain (see page 113), mark out two shoulder facings on the fabric. Each one should be the length of the shoulder seam and 1¼ in. (3 cm) wide, plus a ⅜-in. (1-cm) seam allowance all around. Draw two rectangles to these measurements and cut out.

Make shoulder facing

grain line

Length of shoulder seam

STEP 4

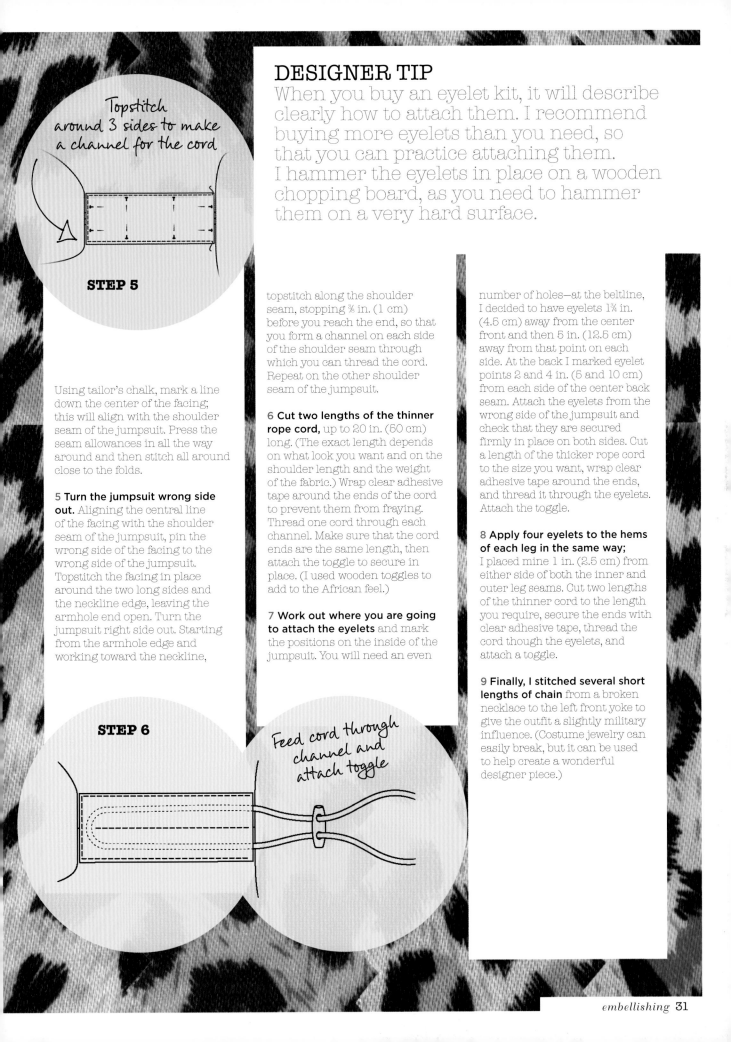

Topstitch around 3 sides to make a channel for the cord

STEP 5

DESIGNER TIP
When you buy an eyelet kit, it will describe clearly how to attach them. I recommend buying more eyelets than you need, so that you can practice attaching them. I hammer the eyelets in place on a wooden chopping board, as you need to hammer them on a very hard surface.

Using tailor's chalk, mark a line down the center of the facing; this will align with the shoulder seam of the jumpsuit. Press the seam allowances in all the way around and then stitch all around close to the folds.

5 Turn the jumpsuit wrong side out. Aligning the central line of the facing with the shoulder seam of the jumpsuit, pin the wrong side of the facing to the wrong side of the jumpsuit. Topstitch the facing in place around the two long sides and the neckline edge, leaving the armhole end open. Turn the jumpsuit right side out. Starting from the armhole edge and working toward the neckline,

topstitch along the shoulder seam, stopping ⅜ in. (1 cm) before you reach the end, so that you form a channel on each side of the shoulder seam through which you can thread the cord. Repeat on the other shoulder seam of the jumpsuit.

6 Cut two lengths of the thinner rope cord, up to 20 in. (50 cm) long. (The exact length depends on what look you want and on the shoulder length and the weight of the fabric.) Wrap clear adhesive tape around the ends of the cord to prevent them from fraying. Thread one cord through each channel. Make sure that the cord ends are the same length, then attach the toggle to secure in place. (I used wooden toggles to add to the African feel.)

7 Work out where you are going to attach the eyelets and mark the positions on the inside of the jumpsuit. You will need an even

number of holes—at the beltline, I decided to have eyelets 1¾ in. (4.5 cm) away from the center front and then 5 in. (12.5 cm) away from that point on each side. At the back I marked eyelet points 2 and 4 in. (5 and 10 cm) from each side of the center back seam. Attach the eyelets from the wrong side of the jumpsuit and check that they are secured firmly in place on both sides. Cut a length of the thicker rope cord to the size you want, wrap clear adhesive tape around the ends, and thread it through the eyelets. Attach the toggle.

8 Apply four eyelets to the hems of each leg in the same way; I placed mine 1 in. (2.5 cm) from either side of both the inner and outer leg seams. Cut two lengths of the thinner cord to the length you require, secure the ends with clear adhesive tape, thread the cord though the eyelets, and attach a toggle.

9 Finally, I stitched several short lengths of chain from a broken necklace to the left front yoke to give the outfit a slightly military influence. (Costume jewelry can easily break, but it can be used to help create a wonderful designer piece.)

STEP 6

Feed cord through channel and attach toggle

Sailor dress

This vintage shift dress had started to disintegrate, with holes appearing in the waistband and around the armholes. I made it into a workable piece of clothing by replacing the front waistband panel with a coordinating piece of denim.

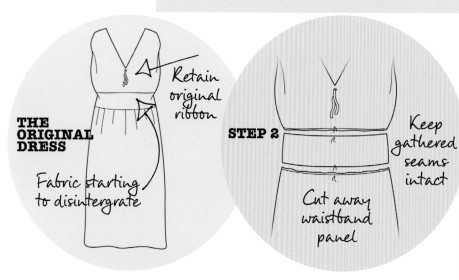

THE ORIGINAL DRESS

Retain original ribbon

Fabric starting to disintergrate

STEP 2

Keep gathered seams intact

Cut away waistband panel

The red ribbon was a feature on the original dress that I wanted to keep. I also felt that the red, white, and blue color scheme created a nautical feel—hence the name of the project!

The dress that I used had a waistband panel on the front, but not on the back.

YOU WILL NEED
- Dress with wide waistband panel
- 40 in. (1 m) stretch denim
- Two metal D-rings
- Approx. 15 in. (38 cm) seam tape
- 3¾ yd (3 m) bias binding, ¾ in. (2 cm) wide
- Brooch

Take ⅝-in. (1.5-cm) seam allowances throughout, unless otherwise stated.

1 **Unpick the waist tie** from the left side seam of the dress. Put it to one side, as you will be using it later.

2 **Work tailor's tacks on the waistband panel and on the skirt** and bodice sections to mark the center front of the panel, top and bottom. Turn the dress inside out

and unpick the waistband panel at the side seams. Cut away the waistband panel, cutting as close to the bodice and skirt seams as possible. Turn the waistband panel right side up and press.

3 **Put the waistband panel right side down on paper and draw around it,** adding a ¾-in. (2-cm) seam allowance all around to compensate for the excess that you cut off at the panel seams. Mark the tailor's tacks on your pattern, too. Pin the paper pattern to the denim fabric on the cross grain (see page 113) and cut out two panels. Work tailor's tacks at the marked points.

4 **With wrong sides together,** machine straight stitch the two denim waistband panels together. Zigzag stitch all around the raw edges and snip off the corners. Turn right side out.

5 **Turn under and press the raw edges of the bodice and skirt** sections along the seam line. Aligning the balance marks, pin the waistband panel to the wrong side of the dress. Baste (tack) in place and then machine stitch all the way around. Zigzag stitch the raw edges of the seam allowance together and press toward the side seams. Check that the waistband panel sits correctly on the front of the dress.

6 **Take the waist tie** still attached to the right side seam of the dress across the center of the denim waistband. Pin and baste (tack)

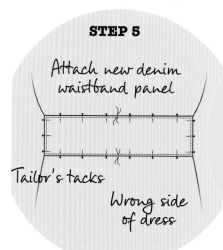

STEP 5

Attach new denim waistband panel

Tailor's tacks

Wrong side of dress

STEP 6

Pin, baste, and topstitch waist tie in place

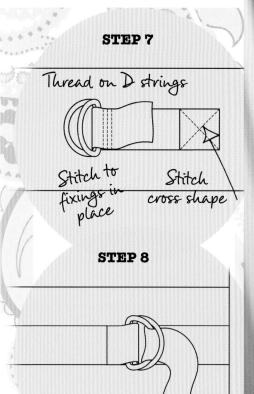

Thread on D strings

Stitch to fixings in place

Stitch cross shape

STEP 8

Thread waist tie through D strings

in place. Topstitch along the top and bottom edges until you reach the end of the tie.

7 Cut the remaining waist tie in half. Position one piece over the tie you've just topstitched and stitch a cross shape over the right-hand end, as shown. Thread both D-rings onto the loose end of the tie, then pull the tie taut to form a loop. Stitch across the tie two or three times to fix the rings securely in place. Cut off any excess tie. Fold the tie with the D-rings back over to the right.

8 Unpick a small section in the left side seam of the waistband panel. From the right side, insert one end of the remaining tie into the gap and pin in place. Turn the dress inside out, then re-stitch the gap, catching the ends of the ties in the stitching. Turn right side out and thread this tie through the D-rings.

9 To make the pockets, draw a box on paper and draw an oval pocket shape within the box. My pocket opening was 6 in. (15 cm)

long and the pocket was 5½ in. (14 cm) at the widest point. Add a ⅝-in. (1.5-cm) seam allowance to the straight side. Fold the denim fabric in half and cut out two pocket shapes for each pocket.

STYLIST'S TIP
To reduce the weight and bulk, cut the pocket from a medium-weight cotton fabric. You will need about 10 in. (25 cm) of fabric for this.

10 Using tailor's chalk, mark the top and bottom of the pocket opening on the side seam of the dress (the pocket should start about 2–3 in. (5–8 cm) below the bottom of the waistband panel. Unpick the side seams of the skirt between the marked points and about 1 in. (2.5 cm) on either side.

SEWING TIP
To make things easier, cut two in-seam pockets from an old pair of jeans and use those!

STEP 11

Stitch seam tape to front pocket opening

11 Cut two pieces of seam tape 2 in. (5 cm) longer than the pocket opening. Place one length on the wrong side of the front pocket seam line, centering it next to the marked points for the pocket opening. Stitch it to the front pocket fabric only.

12 Place the right side of the front pocket on the right side of the skirt front, aligning the top and bottom with the marked points, and pin in place. Machine stitch along the pocket opening. Fold the pocket away from the skirt

STEP 12a

Pin right side of pocket on right side of skirt

Machine stitch along pocket opening

STEP 12b

Fold along stitching line

Fold pocket away from skirt and press

---

along the stitching line and press. Repeat to stitch the back pocket to the back of the skirt.

13 Turn the dress wrong side out. Pin the unpicked side seams and the front and back pocket pieces, right sides together. Baste (tack) the pocket opening closed, basting the pocket opening from dot to dot. Stitch down the side seam as far as the start of the pocket opening, then around the curve of the pocket, and finally down the remaining unpicked section of the side seam, reverse stitching at the start and finish to strengthen the joins. Trim

the seam allowance of the pocket, then zigzag stitch the edges together.

14 Press the side seams open, then press the pocket toward the front of the dress. Repeat steps 10–13 to make the other in-seam pocket.

15 Bind the armholes and neckline (see page 119). I used navy blue satin fabric for the binding and made the neckline binding narrower than that on the armholes.

16 Attach a brooch to the center back waistband to gather the dress in at the waist a little. This is a useful and decorative method for taking in dresses and tops without having to make a permanent alteration.

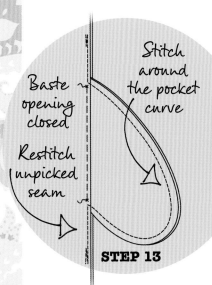

Baste opening closed

Restitch unpicked seam

Stitch around the pocket curve

STEP 13

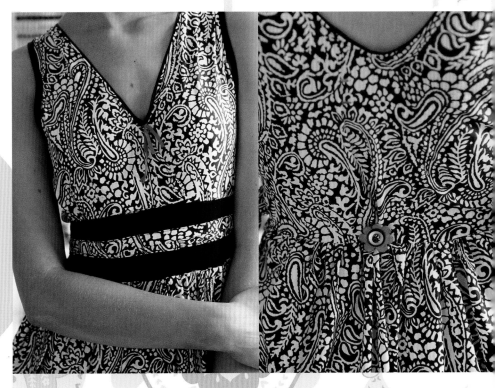

Chapter 2
Reworking

"Reworking" means drastically changing the purpose of the garment—for example, making a simple scarf into a trendy top (see pages 38-43), or transforming one garment into no less than three different items—a fitted skirt, a top, and pull-on cuffs—as I did with the 1980s peplum dress on page 62. There are many reasons for doing this: it could be to update your clothes or simply to tailor them to your body shape or lifestyle. It also fits with my belief that you should always get as much mileage out of one item of clothing as possible. So open up your closet doors, pull out all those unworn or forgotten garments, and open your eyes to their potential. You may be surprised at what you can achieve!

Backless scarf top with ribbon ties

This simple yet effective project can take as little as ten minutes. All you need is a square vintage scarf and ribbon for the ties; it is useful to use a ribbon that looks the same on both sides.

Mark the tie positions in chalk

Machine stitch the scarf edge

RS of scarf

Fold the ribbon back on itself and stitch again

STEP 2

YOU WILL NEED
- Scarf approx. 40 in. (100 cm) square
- 2½ yd (2.25 m) narrow ribbon for the ties
- Tailor's chalk
- Ruler

Take ¼-in. (6-mm) seam allowances throughout, unless otherwise stated.

1 Cut three 30-in. (75-cm) lengths of ribbon. Cut each length exactly in half.

2 Lay the scarf flat, right side down. On opposite sides of the scarf, using tailor's chalk, mark three evenly spaced points for the ribbon ties. Pin three lengths of ribbon to each side of the scarf, centering them on the marked points and aligning the raw ends with the scarf edge. Machine or hand stitch the ribbon in place, stitching ⅜ in. (1 cm) from the scarf edge. Fold the ribbon back on itself and stitch across it again, as close to the scarf edge as possible.

3 Cut the ends of the ribbon into a V-shape to prevent fraying.

STYLIST TIP
If you don't want to go braless, why not wear a bikini top underneath as an added feature?

DESIGNER TIP
Why not stitch a bead to the end of each piece of ribbon? This will add more weight and more style!

This is a great vacation top as it's loose (and therefore cool) and will protect your shoulders from sunburn. I made this one from a vintage scarf, but you could make it from scratch by hemming a square of your favorite fabric if you prefer.

YOU WILL NEED
• Scarf approx. 40 in. (100 cm) square
• Set square
• Tailor's chalk

1 **Check the hem of the scarf** to find out which is the wrong side. Lay the scarf wrong side up and mark the central point with tailor's chalk.

2 **The square cut out of the center of the scarf** will be your neckline, so take your time measuring, cutting, and stitching as you want it to look nice and neat. Measure and mark 3 in. (7.5 cm) out from the central point in each direction and draw a square in tailor's chalk. Measure and mark another line ⅝ in. (1.5 cm) beyond this to give a 7-in. (18-cm) square.

3 **Set your machine to a long stitch** and stitch all around the marked 7-in. (18-cm) square, just inside the drawn line, to help prevent fraying.

4 **Cut the 6-in. (15-cm) square out of the center of the scarf.** Snip into each corner, taking care not to cut through the stitching, and press under to help form a hem.

5 **Roll the edge of the fabric inward** to make a very narrow hem and pin all around. Using a flat hemming stitch (see page 109), sew all the way around the square.

6 **Place a piece** of cotton fabric on top, press gently on a cool setting, and you're good to go!

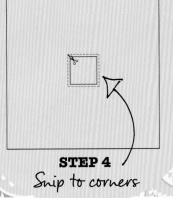

STEP 2
Measure central square

STEP 4
Snip to corners

DESIGNER TIP
For a little weight and individuality, add some detail to the hemline of the scarf. In this project, I have sewn sequins on for a more dressed-up look.

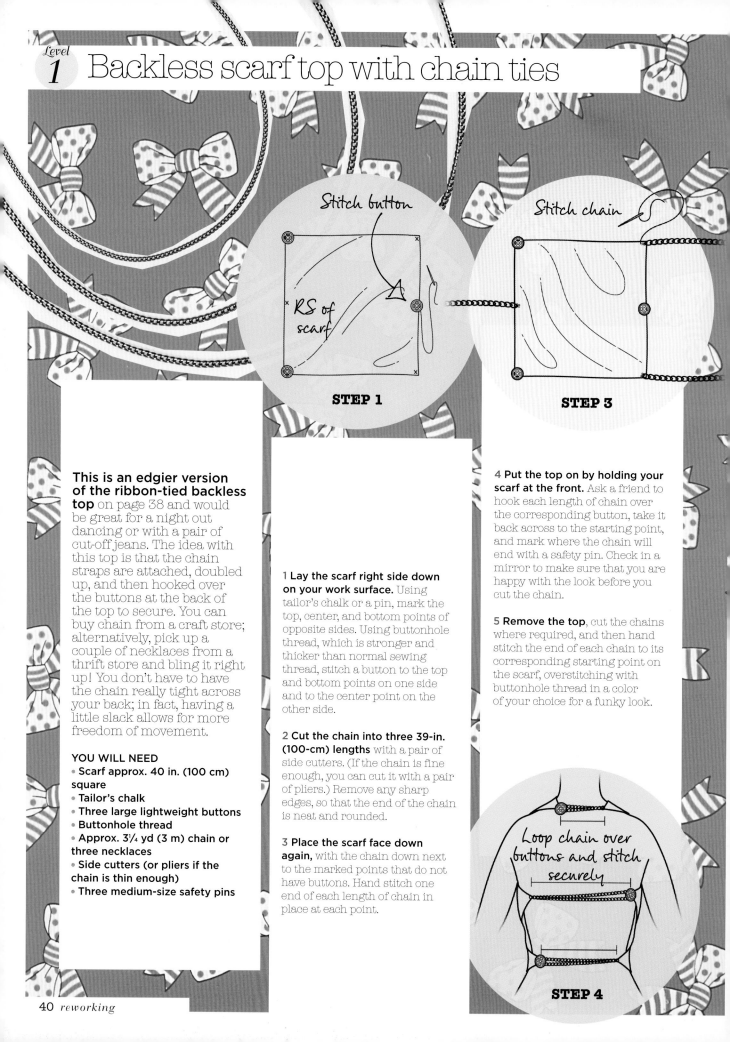

Backless scarf top with chain ties

Stitch button

RS of scarf

STEP 1

Stitch chain

STEP 3

This is an edgier version of the ribbon-tied backless top on page 38 and would be great for a night out dancing or with a pair of cut-off jeans. The idea with this top is that the chain straps are attached, doubled up, and then hooked over the buttons at the back of the top to secure. You can buy chain from a craft store; alternatively, pick up a couple of necklaces from a thrift store and bling it right up! You don't have to have the chain really tight across your back; in fact, having a little slack allows for more freedom of movement.

YOU WILL NEED
• Scarf approx. 40 in. (100 cm) square
• Tailor's chalk
• Three large lightweight buttons
• Buttonhole thread
• Approx. 3¼ yd (3 m) chain or three necklaces
• Side cutters (or pliers if the chain is thin enough)
• Three medium-size safety pins

1 **Lay the scarf right side down on your work surface.** Using tailor's chalk or a pin, mark the top, center, and bottom points of opposite sides. Using buttonhole thread, which is stronger and thicker than normal sewing thread, stitch a button to the top and bottom points on one side and to the center point on the other side.

2 **Cut the chain into three 39-in. (100-cm) lengths** with a pair of side cutters. (If the chain is fine enough, you can cut it with a pair of pliers.) Remove any sharp edges, so that the end of the chain is neat and rounded.

3 **Place the scarf face down again,** with the chain down next to the marked points that do not have buttons. Hand stitch one end of each length of chain in place at each point.

4 **Put the top on by holding your scarf at the front.** Ask a friend to hook each length of chain over the corresponding button, take it back across to the starting point, and mark where the chain will end with a safety pin. Check in a mirror to make sure that you are happy with the look before you cut the chain.

5 **Remove the top,** cut the chains where required, and then hand stitch the end of each chain to its corresponding starting point on the scarf, overstitching with buttonhole thread in a color of your choice for a funky look.

Loop chain over buttons and stitch securely

STEP 4

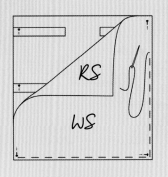

Reversible backless top

Pin ribbon to marked points

RS of scarf

STEP 2

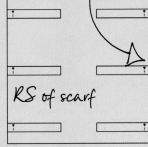

RS

WS

STEP 3

If you want to get even more mileage out of your **scarf top,** why not make it reversible? This would be useful for a trip where you want to pack lightly but have two looks in one—perhaps you are at a festival or need a day-to-night look that takes up little space. It is important to use fabrics of a similar weight for the two sides of the top. As in the Backless Scarf Top on page 38, use ribbon that looks the same on both sides for the ties.

YOU WILL NEED
• **Two 40-in. (100-cm) scarves or hemmed squares of fabric**
• **2½ yd (2.25 m) ribbon**
• **Tailor's chalk**
• **Ruler**

Take ¼-in. (6-mm) seam allowances throughout, unless otherwise stated

1 Cut three 30-in. (75-cm) lengths of ribbon. Cut each length exactly in half. Place one scarf or piece of fabric right side up on your work surface. Using tailor's chalk, mark three evenly spaced points for the ribbon ties on opposite sides of the scarf, marking the width of the ribbon each time .

2 Centering them on the marked points and aligning the raw ends with the scarf edge, pin one ribbon to each marked point, facing in toward the center.

3 Place the second scarf or piece of fabric right side down on top. Pin the two layers together at each corner to secure, inserting the pins lengthwise. Baste (tack) the pieces together, stitching as close to the edge as possible.

SEWING TIP
Pins can leave holes, particularly in fine fabrics such as silk, so insert the pins lengthwise, as close to the hem as possible, as shown in the illustration. Any holes will then be hidden in the seam allowance when the pieces are stitched together.

4 Machine stitch all around, reverse stitching at the start and finish and leaving a 3-in. (8-cm) gap in one edge. Turn right side out and press flat. Turn the edges of the gap under and oversew (see page 109) by hand to close.

5 Topstitch all the way around, matching the bobbin thread color to the underside of the scarf and the top thread to the top of the scarf. I then machined around some of the flowers on each side to help prevent the two layers of silk from sliding around.

6 Cut the ends of the ribbons into a V-shape to prevent fraying.

Backless sequinned dress

Transform yourself into the hottest girl in town with this fabulous little black dress made from a sparkly sequinned top.

Don't waste a scrap of this wonderful sparkly fabric!

Once you have removed the back of the top, use the cut-off section to add a little vintage glamour to a tired sweater (see page 22). You'll need to use heavy-duty machine needles for this project, as they can easily break on sequinned fabric.

YOU WILL NEED
- Vintage sequinned top (the bigger the better!)
- 2¼ yd (2 m) cotton tape, ⅝ in. (1.5 cm) wide, to match the top
- Coordinating scarf with stretch, at least 4 in. (10 cm) wide, or other trim of your choice
- Two 40-in. (1-m) lengths each of two colors of stringed sequins (I chose silver and black)
- Buttonhole thread for hook and eyes, and machine thread
- Hook-and-eye fastener (size 3)

Take ⅝-in. (1.5-cm) seam allowances throughout, unless otherwise stated.

1 Put the top on in front of a full-length mirror. Decide how deep you want the V-shaped backless section to be and ask a friend to insert a pin at the lowest point of the "V." (Here, the bottom of the V-shape was pinned across the back zipper; don't be afraid to cut into a zipline if necessary— see page 124.) The high points of the "V" are the back neckline, so ask your friend to pin across the shoulder seams at these points, too.

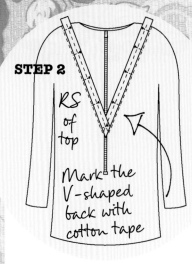

STEP 2

RS of top

Mark the V-shaped back with cotton tape

2 Lay the top face down on your work surface, with any fastenings done up. Tailor's chalk does not work well on sequinned fabric, so use cotton tape to mark out the V-shape on the back. Measure the tape on both sides of the V-shape to make sure they are the same length. Pin the tape in place, making sure it is taut: the bottom edge of the tape indicates where you want the V-shape to end while the top edge marks the cutting line. Mark the front neckline in the same way, so that front and back align at the shoulder seams. Baste (tack) below the bottom edge of the tape all the way along the neckline and backless section, as this marks the seam allowance.

3 If your top does not have a zipper, omit this step. If it does have a zipper, undo it. Using matching buttonhole thread, oversew the zipper on each side

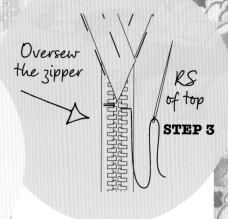

Oversew the zipper

RS of top

STEP 3

between the teeth at the base of the "V" so that, once you have cut off the excess, the zipper pull will not come off. Using buttonhole thread, sew on a hook-and-eye fastener to secure.

4 Starting at the neckline, cut along the top edge of the cotton tape with a pair of long-handled scissors. Remove the cotton tape. Using a small pair of scissors and following the basting (tacking) line from step 2, remove the sequins from the seam allowance, front and back.

STEP 4

Cut the V-shape

RS of top

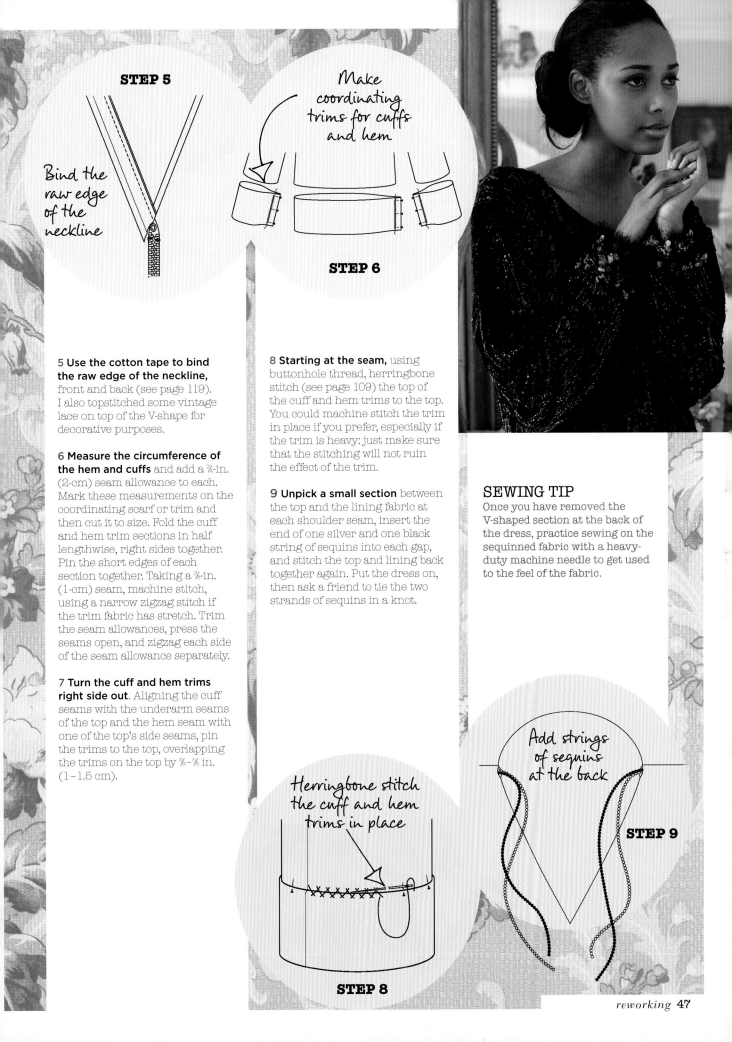

Bind the raw edge of the neckline

Make coordinating trims for cuffs and hem

5 Use the cotton tape to bind the raw edge of the neckline, front and back (see page 119). I also topstitched some vintage lace on top of the V-shape for decorative purposes.

6 Measure the circumference of the hem and cuffs and add a ¾-in. (2-cm) seam allowance to each. Mark these measurements on the coordinating scarf or trim and then cut it to size. Fold the cuff and hem trim sections in half lengthwise, right sides together. Pin the short edges of each section together. Taking a ⅜-in. (1-cm) seam, machine stitch, using a narrow zigzag stitch if the trim fabric has stretch. Trim the seam allowances, press the seams open, and zigzag each side of the seam allowance separately.

7 Turn the cuff and hem trims right side out. Aligning the cuff seams with the underarm seams of the top and the hem seam with one of the top's side seams, pin the trims to the top, overlapping the trims on the top by ⅜–⅝ in. (1–1.5 cm).

8 Starting at the seam, using buttonhole thread, herringbone stitch (see page 109) the top of the cuff and hem trims to the top. You could machine stitch the trim in place if you prefer, especially if the trim is heavy: just make sure that the stitching will not ruin the effect of the trim.

9 Unpick a small section between the top and the lining fabric at each shoulder seam, insert the end of one silver and one black string of sequins into each gap, and stitch the top and lining back together again. Put the dress on, then ask a friend to tie the two strands of sequins in a knot.

SEWING TIP

Once you have removed the V-shaped section at the back of the dress, practice sewing on the sequinned fabric with a heavy-duty machine needle to get used to the feel of the fabric.

Herringbone stitch the cuff and hem trims in place

Add strings of sequins at the back

Two-piece sweater conversion

Level 2

Sweaters are not only practical but look great, too—and worn ones don't need to be thrown in the trash. A good piece of knitwear can be converted into many useful things—a cozy cushion cover, a beanie hat... the list is endless. For these two projects, you will need a long-sleeved sweater.

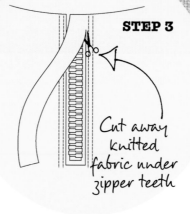

STEP 3

Cut away knitted fabric under zipper teeth

It's important to use a ballpoint needle for this project, as the sweater fabric will have some stretch. What drew me to this sweater was the bright colors. I felt that adding the deep blue metal zippers would bring out the vibrant orange even more. The zippers on the sleeves are for decorative purposes only, but the zips on the neckline can be worn open and closed.

YOU WILL NEED
- Mediumweight wool-mix sweater
- Two 4-in. (10-cm) metal zippers
- 18-in. (45-cm) heavy open-ended plastic zipper
- Matching and contrasting machine thread
- Ballpoint machine needle
- Zipper foot

1 First of all, work out where you want the zippers to go. I added them to the neckline, as I wanted it to be possible for the sweater to be worn with the zippers either open or closed. You could also insert them on the hemline, at the side seams.

2 Lay the sweater on your work surface, with the front facing up. Pin, then baste (tack) the short metal zippers in place at the neckline, folding the tape ends over to the wrong side for a neat finish. Using a zipper foot, machine stitch the zippers in place (see page 125). If your zipper tape is wide, you will need to sew two parallel lines ¼ in. (5 mm) apart. My first stitching line was ⅜ in. (1 cm) away from the zipper teeth.

3 Cut away a small section of knitted fabric under the zipper teeth, cutting as close to the stitched line as possible.

4 Using tailor's chalk, draw a line all around the sleeve ¼ in. (6 mm) below the armhole seam. Cut the sleeves off at this point and put them to one side to use for the headband (see page 50). Staystitch around the armhole so that that the fabric does not unravel or stretch when you attach the zipper.

5 Undo the open-ended zipper and separate the two halves. Measure the circumference of the armhole and add 1 in. (2.5 cm). Cut the two halves of the zipper to this length, cutting off the excess at both the top and the bottom of the zipper halves (see page 124). Starting from the underarm/side seam, aligning the tape side of the zipper with the raw edges of the armhole, pin and baste (tack) one half of the zipper around the sleeve line on the right side of the sweater. The zipper teeth will protrude beyond the edge of the armhole.

STEP 5

Pin and baste zipper around armhole

STEP 6

Cut off zipper where the ends overlap

6 Where the two ends meet, cut off the required number of teeth from one end of the zipper and overlap the other end on top. Using a zipper foot and matching thread, machine stitch the zipper in place. Attach the other half of the zipper to the other armhole in the same way.

DESIGNER TIP

I used a funky, contrasting orange thread for topstitching. I also faced the armhole with 2-in. (5-cm) wide cotton tape to create a neat edge and emphasize the shape.

1940s-style headband

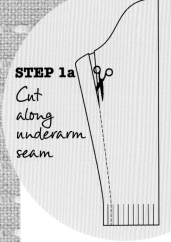

STEP 1a
Cut along underarm seam

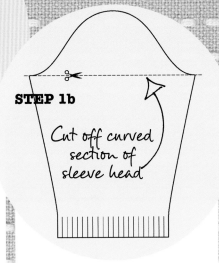

STEP 1b
Cut off curved section of sleeve head

I made the cut-off sleeves of the same sweater into a 1940s-style workwear headband for a funky, vintage look. If you are not confident about matching up the pattern, use a plain sweater! This is a perfect recycling project if you have a sweater that has more holes in it than a sieve, but whose sleeves are still intact. It is also a great look on a bad hair day!

YOU WILL NEED
- Sleeves from the sweater
- Decorative vintage button
- Matching machine thread
- Buttonhole thread
- Ballpoint machine needle

Take ³⁄₈-in. (1-cm) seam allowances throughout.

1 Cut off the sleeves just below the armhole seam. Cut along the armhole seams of the sleeves, open up the sleeves, and lay them flat on your work surface. Using a set square or a ruler and tailor's chalk, draw a straight line across the sleeve below the sleeve head and cut off the curved section.

2 Lay the sleeves wrong side up on your work surface, as shown, and match up any pattern. Place the two sleeves right sides together and pin along the short raw edge, inserting the pins parallel to the short edge. Open up the sleeve again and check that the pattern matches across

the two halves. Baste (tack) the two sleeves together along the short raw edge. Using a ballpoint needle and a narrow zigzag stitch, reverse stitching at the start and finish, machine stitch the sleeves together.

3 This seam will be sitting at the back of your head, so you want it to be nice and flat. Zigzag stitch each side of the seam allowance separately, and then press the seam open.

Align any pattern then pin and stitch

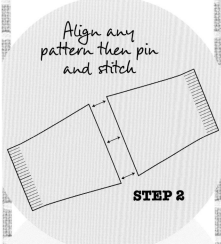

STEP 2

Stitch to form a tube

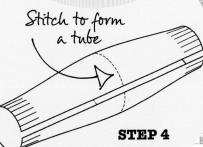

STEP 4

4 Fold the fabric in half lengthwise, right sides together, and pin along the long raw edge. Using a ballpoint needle and a narrow zigzag stitch, reverse stitching at the start and finish, machine stitch along the long raw edge to form a tube. Zigzag each side of the seam allowance separately to prevent fraying, then press the seam open. Turn right side out.

5 Place the headband around your head and tie in a knot at the front. Carefully remove the headband, keeping hold of the knot. Pin the knot in place. Fold the excess fabric under, so that it sits on the back of the headband, and pin in place: the aim is for the knot to have a neat, flat bottom. Oversew the excess fabric in place.

6 Using a doubled length of buttonhole thread, stitch through the center of the knot several times to secure it in place. (Don't worry if your stitches are not very neat, as they will be covered by the button.) Stitch your chosen button on top of the knot. I used a contrasting color of thread, as this can look funky and fun. If your button has four holes, working a cross stitch through the holes is very much in keeping with the 1940s look.

STYLIST'S TIP
Opt for a brooch rather than a button; this will free you up to create different looks with one headband.

Circus skirt

Maxi skirts can occasionally feel restricting. If you want to show the world your new boots or run for a bus (or both!), this skirt could be for you.

You don't even need an overlocker for this project—just use zigzag stitch to work with the stretch of the fabric. I wanted to create the feel of a trapeze artist's skirt.

YOU WILL NEED
- Woollen maxi skirt
- Tailor's chalk
- Soft net cut into strips 3 in. (7.5 cm) wide
- 3 yd (3 m) ribbon, $\frac{3}{8}$ in. (1 cm) wide
- Six vintage buttons in varying sizes
- Matching machine thread
- Buttonhole thread to match skirt
- Small weight (optional)

1 Put the skirt on in front of a full-length mirror. If possible, ask a friend to pin it at the front to the length you want. You could also do this yourself, but be careful with the pins. If you want to alter the back length, mark that with pins, too.

2 Fold the skirt in half down the center front, right sides together. Lay it flat on your work surface and mark where you intend to cut the front, using tailor's chalk. Carefully cut along your drawn line, cutting through both layers of the front at once so that the left and right sides are symmetrical. Repeat on the back of the skirt; here, I also cut a small split in the center back to make walking easier, hemming it with a zigzag stitch.

SEWING TIP
Another option is to make paper templates for the shapes you want to cut out of the front and back of the skirt, pin them in place, and chalk around them.

3 Stay stitch approximately $\frac{5}{8}$ in. (1.5 cm) up from the cut edge to prevent the skirt from stretching.

4 Measure the hem of the skirt and double this measurement. Cut a strip of net to this length and 3 in. (7.5 cm) wide; the extra length is allow for the pleating. You may have to sew several strips of net together to get the length you need, but the seams will be hidden in the pleating in the next step.

STEP 6

Add buttons and a vintage weight

5 Now turn the skirt inside out. Starting from the split at the back of the skirt, place the net strip on the hem and machine stitch it in place with a narrow zigzag stitch, stitching about ⅜ in. (1 cm) from the edge and gently pleating the net with your fingertips as you go. Don't worry about making the pleats uniform in size: the more random the better! If you don't feel confident about doing this "freehand," then pin or even baste (tack) the pleats in place before machine stitching.

6 Turn the skirt right side out again. Add detail to the back of the skirt (in this example, where the split is) by sewing on vintage buttons. I also added a small vintage weight to the hem to replace the original bottom button to make the skirt hang better. I used buttonhole thread for this to help hold the weight.

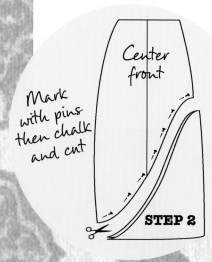

Mark with pins then chalk and cut

Center front

STEP 2

STEP 5

Pleat as you stitch

STEP 8

Sew coordinating buttons on top of ribbon

7 Pin ribbon around the hem over the stitching line of the net and zigzag stitch in place, using a contrasting color of thread if you wish.

DESIGNER TIP

When deciding on which side of the skirt to sew the buttons, think about side you wear your bag. If your bag hangs over the buttons, it may wear them down or cause them to dig into you.

8 Cut a strip of net 1¼ in. (3 cm) wide. Lay the strip approximately 2 in. (5 cm) below the top of the skirt and machine stitch along the center to fix it in place. Stitch ribbon over the top of the net, turning the ends under to finish them off neatly. Sew three coordinating buttons on top of the ribbon on the front of the skirt, slightly off-center, as a finishing touch.

DESIGNER TIP This skirt is an ideal day-to-night number! Just change your pantyhose and throw on some heeled shoe boots for a show-stopping look.

Boyfriend shirt tunic

This project is particularly useful if you are on a budget, as you can usually buy shirts very cheaply in thrift or charity stores.

Alternatively, if your partner is having a clear-out, why not take one of his shirts? This shirt dress can be worn with leggings, tights, pants, or even on the beach.

YOU WILL NEED
- Large shirt, ideally with a dress-shirt double cuff
- Tailor's dummy
- Matching machine thread
- Vintage buttons to fit the buttonholes of the original shirt
- 2 yd (2 m) elastic, ⅜ in. (1 cm) wide

Take ⅝-in. (1.5-cm) seam allowances throughout, unless otherwise stated.

1 Remove the pocket from the shirt front with an unpicker or small sharp scissors and press the stitching marks out.

2 Button the shirt, place it on a tailor's dummy, and mark the start and finish of up to seven pintucks on each side of the front, using tailor's chalk or pins. My pintucks were spaced ⅜ in. (1 cm) apart and were about 25 cm (10 in.) long, measuring down from the shoulder seam. Fold and press the fabric so that the top and bottom marks of the first pintuck align, then machine stitch as close to the fold as possible, using matching thread. Repeat until you have stitched all the pintucks, then press the pintucks toward the side seams of the body.

STEP 2

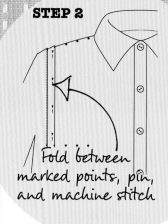

Fold between marked points, pin, and machine stitch

STEP 3

Topstitch the center front placket

STEP 5

Stretch the elastic to the required length, then zigzag stich in place

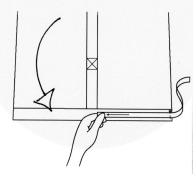

3 Topstitch up the center front of the shirt from the hemline along the existing stitch lines of the center front placket for about 6 in. (15 cm) in order to close up the lower part of the shirt. Lay the shirt flat and cut the back hemline level with the front (as men's shirts tend to be longer at the back).

4 Unpick the hem. Fold over a ¾-in. (2-cm) double hem and press. Machine stitch as close as possible to the folded-over edge.

5 Measure the length of the hem, divide by four, and cut two pieces of elastic to this length. Find the center of the first piece of elastic and pin it over one side seam. Stretch one end of the elastic out with your fingers until it reaches halfway across the front, then zigzag stitch it in place. Stretch the other end halfway across the back and zigzag in place. Repeat with the other length of elastic at the other side of the shirt.

SEWING TIP
For a tulip-shaped shirt, leave a gap in one side seam when you stitch the hem and thread a single length of elastic all the way through the hem (see page 122), securing the ends by working a few hand stitches over them.

6 Change the buttons if you wish—but keep to the same size as the buttons that were originally on the shirt so that they fit the buttonholes.

7 Cut the cuffs off the sleeves of the shirt. Turn up a narrow

DESIGNER TIP
If you're using a plain white skirt for this project, why not dye it, too (see page 126)? You can also vary the buttons used for extra color and detail.

double hem on the sleeves and press. Machine stitch close to the turned-up edge. You can then choose whether to wear the sleeves down or rolled up with the tab detail.

8 Cut one of the cuffs in half lengthwise. Turn under the raw edges all around, press, and topstitch all around to create two tabs for the sleeve straps.

9 Turn the sleeves inside out. Machine stitch one tab to each arm, about halfway down the

upper arm. Turn the sleeves right side out again. Roll the sleeves up to the required depth and attach a button to the outer sleeve. Use the buttonhole on the tab to hold the sleeves at the required depth.

10 Put the shirt back on the tailor's dummy and work down from the yoke. Cut the remaining cuff in half lengthwise, as in step 7, and make a tab. Unpick a small section at the bottom of the yoke at the center back, slide one end of the tab underneath, and re-stitch. Stitch two tucks on either side of the tab, as in step 1. Attach a button to correspond with the buttonhole in the tab. (I used a cufflink-style vintage button to offset the feminine look of the shirt dress.)

WS of shirt

Stitch tab to upper arm

STEP 9a

RS of shirt

STEP 9b

Button on outer sleeve

Cut the cuff in half lengthwise

STEP 8a

STEP 8b

Turn the raw edges under

Topstitch to create tabs

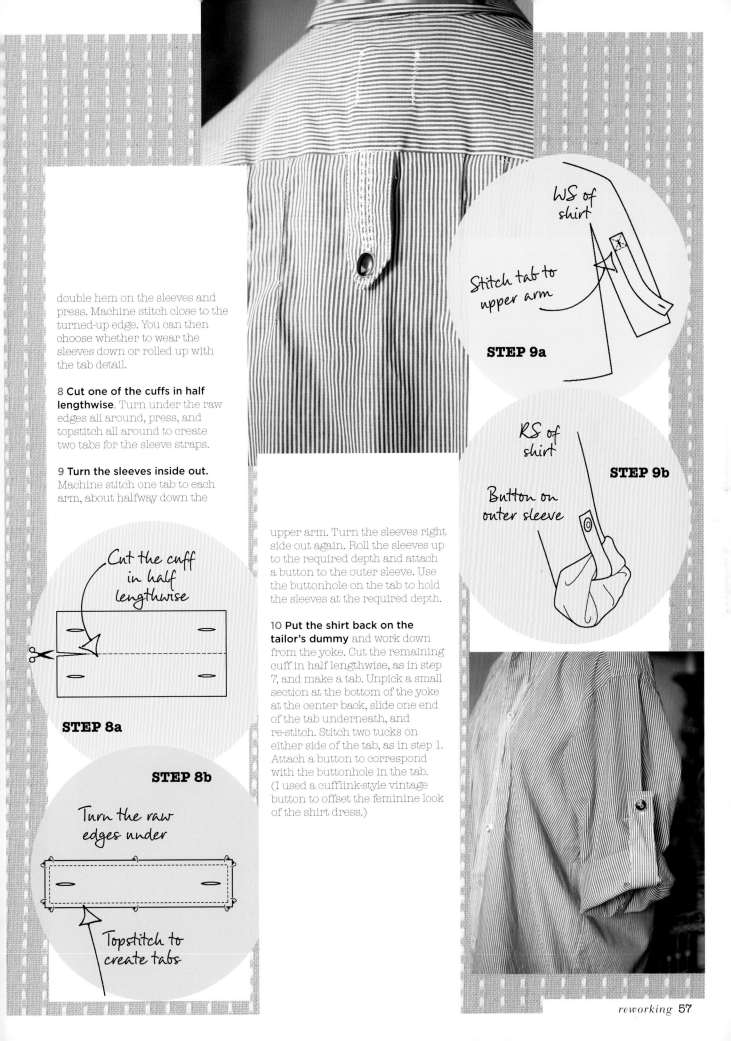

Bling top

This 1980s polyester, gold-spotted number had great potential. To make it look more couture than costume, I had to make a few little changes...

Dated neckline

Boxy shoulder pads

THE ORIGINAL TOP

Cut bodice panel at an angle

STEP 4

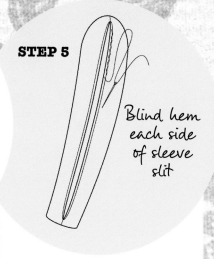

STEP 5

Blind hem each side of sleeve slit

YOU WILL NEED
• One tie knot top, preferably with two-piece sleeves so that there is an outer sleeve seam
• 12-in. (30-cm) metal zipper
• Decorative woven knot or woven frog clasp
• Matching thread
• Ballpoint needle
• Zipper foot
• Two buttons that fit through the knot of the frog clasp

Take ⅝-in. (1.5-cm) seam allowances throughout, unless otherwise stated.

1 Turn the top inside out and remove the shoulder pads. (They were easy to snip off in this case, as they were simply stitched on at either end.)

2 Turn the top right side out and locate the knot seam. Unpick the seam, then untie the knot so that the fabric hangs down both sides of the center front. Unpick the rest of the center front seam, excluding the neckband.

3 Turn the top right side out and put it on a tailor's dummy. Cut the right front bodice panel at an angle. Hem the raw edges of the bodice front.

4 Lay the top flat, right side up, with the zipper beneath it, directly below the center front collar. Pin the edges of the zipper in place, in line with the existing seam line. Baste (tack), then machine stitch the zipper in place from the wrong side.

5 Now create the slashed sleeves. Turn the top inside out. On the outer arm seams, make a tailor's chalk mark ⅜ in. (1 cm) down from the end of each shoulder seam. Insert a pin across the seam at this point to prevent the seam from unraveling. Repeat this process ⅜ in. (1 cm) up from the top of the cuff. Unpick the outer arm seams between the pinned points. Press the seam allowances back in place and then blind hem (see page 109)

by hand or by machine, so that no stitches are visible on the right side of the fabric. If you wish, you can topstitch the seams in a matching or a contrasting color of thread.

6 Turn the top right side out and put it back on. Ask a friend to pin the cuffs tightly around your wrist. Remove the existing buttons from the cuffs. Attach a woven knot or frog clasp and a button to each cuff to create a more tailored look.

STEP 6

Nip in cuffs with frog clasp and button

Drop-back top

This stunning floral print dress had a divine combination of colors, yet the shape felt frumpy. It needed a lift. The answer (for me!) was to cut it down to a top and to bring out the blue tone by applying a blue satin binding.

STEP 2

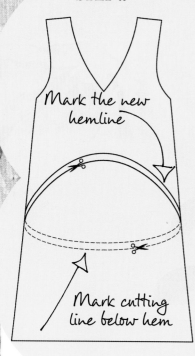

Mark the new hemline

Mark cutting line below hem

I cut the top shorter at the front than at the back for an edgier, more contemporary look; it can be worn either way around. This is a great way to rework an oversized secondhand dress whose fabric you love.

YOU WILL NEED
• **Dress** (oversized is fine)
• **30 in. (75 cm) bias binding,** ⅝ in. (1.5 cm) wide, to bind the inner side seams
• **2¼ yd (2 m) satin bias binding,** ⅝ in. (1.5 cm) wide, for armholes and neckline

Take ⅝-in. (1.5-cm) seam allowances throughout, unless otherwise stated.

1 **Put the dress on in front of a full-length mirror.** As with the Circus Skirt (page 52), pin where you want the hemline to be both at the front and the back. (Ask a friend to help.) It is also useful to mark the lowest point of the hem on each side seam, as they need to be the same length. Take the dress off, turn it inside out, and lay it flat on your work surface, with the front facing up.

2 **Using tailor's chalk,** mark the points you have pinned, then remove the pins. Using the same method as in the Circus Skirt (see page 52), mark the hemline on the front and the back. Draw another line ⅝ in. (1.5 cm) below the hemline; this is your cutting line. Then cut along the cutting line.

3 **Turn the top inside out** and try it on again. If it is too wide across your back, ask a friend to pin the top under your arms at the armhole. Get your friend to pin all the way down the side seams. (You don't have to have the same amount of seam all the way down: just make sure that each side is the same.) Using tailor's chalk, mark a ⅝-in. (1.5-cm) seam allowance all down the pinned side seams. Take the top off.

4 **Baste (tack) along the pinned side seams.** Cut along the marked seam allowance to trim off any excess fabric. Reverse stitching at the start and finish of each side seam, machine stitch the seams.

5 **To secure the stitching, bind the side seams** (see page 119); as the top is a different length at the front and back, part of the inner seam binding will be visible, so I made the binding from a funky vintage print fabric. Turn the top right side out.

6 **Pin, press, and stitch the hemline,** using whichever method you choose (see page 109).

7 **Starting at the shoulder seam,** apply satin bias binding around the neckline of the top (see page 119). Attach a bright button at the center front neckline; this also has the advantage of covering up any untidiness where the two ends of the bias binding meet.

8 **Finally, apply satin bias binding** around the armholes.

DESIGNER'S TIP
Why not topstitch some funky binding to the wrong side of the hemline? If there is a sharp drop in the shape, you may have difficulty making the hem neat, and binding will cover up any mistakes as well as providing a pretty finishing touch.

STEP 4

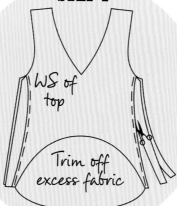

WS of top

Trim off excess fabric

Three from one

This peplum dress is made out of polyester and had the potential to be transformed into three separate items of clothing.

Dated neckline and sleeves

THE ORIGINAL PEPLUM DRESS

YOU WILL NEED
- Peplum skirt, preferably with an elasticated waistband
- Dress or skirt in a coordinating pattern
- Matching machine thread
- Ballpoint machine needle (if the dress is in a stretch fabric such as the polyester used here)
- Pinking shears
- Tracing wheel and carbon paper

Take ⅝-in. (1.5-cm) seam allowances throughout, unless otherwise stated.

1 **Measure, mark, and cut the top of the dress off** ¼ in. (6 mm) above the elastic waistband. Put the top to one side to make the Sweetheart Top (page 64).

2 **Put the skirt on and ask a friend to pin the side seams** to a more fitted shape. (Just lift up the peplum skirt while you do this.) This skirt had four panels. You could, in this instance, roughly pin the two side seams, and then measure and mark accurately once you have laid the skirt out flat. Take a few steps around the room to check that you can, in fact, walk in the skirt before you cut into it.

3 **Take the skirt off and lay it on your work surface, wrong side out.** Measure the difference between the original skirt and your new, pinned side seams at the top and bottom of the seams and make a note of the measurements. Divide these measurements by the number of panels on the skirt to work out how much you need to take off each panel. Turn the skirt wrong side out. Halve the amount you want to take off each panel, then mark this measurement on each seam of each panel, using a rule and tailor's chalk. These will be your new seam lines. Also measure and mark a ⅝-in. (1.5-cm) seam allowance parallel to these seam lines.

SEWING TIP
If the original waist measurement of the skirt is more than 2 in. (5 cm) wider than your waist, you will need to remove the peplum skirt and repeat step 3 with the peplum skirt, so that the waist measurements between the skirt and the peplum match.

Peplum pencil skirt

Level 2

The A-line skirt of the dress needed a bit of nifty tailoring to transform it into something a little more sophisticated. If you like the vintage look, a pencil skirt looks great with a pair of killer anklestrap heels and a little cardigan. You will also be creating a dual-purpose waistband—an exposed waistband like the one shown opposite, and a lower-waisted option (tucking the waistband back into the skirt) for that sometimes much-needed stomach support!

The skirt of this dress had four panels, but the same principles would apply on a dress or skirt with just two panels.

STEP 3

Alter skirt

New seam allowance line

Existing seam between panels

WS

Align
marked
lines and
machine
stitch

*Trim along the seam
allowance line*

WS of
panel

STEP 4

4 Fold adjacent panels right sides together, aligning your marked lines top and bottom, pin and then stitch along your new chalked seam lines. (If the fabric has a stretch to it, use a narrow zigzag stitch and a ballpoint needle.) Cut the excess fabric off by cutting along the marked seam allowance lines with pinking shears for a crisp finish, then press the seams open.

5 Press the seams open, then zigzag stitch the raw edges of the seam allowances separately. Press the seams open again if necessary. Re-stitch the hem at these points so that you have a nice, flat hemline.

6 Put the skirt on to see where it sits on your waist and take this measurement. Then take a depth measurement: how high do you want the skirt waistband to be? Make a paper pattern for the waistband (see page 120), remembering to add a ⅝-in. (1.5-cm) seam allowance all around. Pin the paper pattern to the hemmed (bottom) edge of a coordinating skirt or dress and cut out.

7 With right sides together, pin the unhemmed edge of the waistband to the skirt and stitch in place (see page 121). Fold the hemmed edge over to the wrong side, then zigzag stitch in place.

Sweetheart top

This is a classic feminine top that would complement any look. Sewing a belt into a piece of clothing at the side seams can give it an individual look and help you to accentuate your waist at the same time.

I removed the neck ties from the original top to use as a belt inside the back of the top.

YOU WILL NEED
- **Top removed from the peplum dress (see page 62)**
- **Matching machine thread**
- **Ballpoint machine needle**
- **Elasticated belt**
- **1 yd (1 m) elastic, ¼ in. (6 mm) wide**

1 After you have removed the skirt part of the dress, unpick the neck ties and put them to one side (to use in step 7 for an inner waist belt).

2 Lay the top flat on your work surface, with the front facing up. Measure up from the base of the sleeves to where you want the sleeves to end and mark with tailor's chalk. Draw a line 1 in. (2.5 cm) below the chalk mark, then cut along the marked line. Put the cut-off fabric to one side to use for the ruffled glove cuffs (see page 65).

3 Turn the top wrong side out and turn under the raw edges of the sleeves by ¼ in. (6 mm). Turn up ⅝ in. (1.5 cm) all the way around the sleeve hems, pin in place, and press. Using a narrow zigzag stitch, stitch around the sleeve hems as close to the edge as possible, leaving a 1-in. (2.5-cm) gap at the underarm seams to create a casing (see page 121) for the elastic.

STEP 3
Leave a gap to create a casing for the elastic

Feed the elastic through the casing

STEP 7
Wrong side

Insert the belt

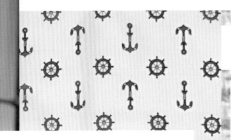

SEWING TIP

All casings should be at least ¼ in. (6 mm) wider than the elastic they are to enclose to allow for its free movement through the fabric tunnel.

4 Measure the circumference of your arm just above the elbow and cut two pieces of elastic to this length. (This allows for a snug fit when the ends of the elastic are overlapped.) Thread the elastic through the sleeve casing (see page 122), then zigzag stitch the gap in the casing closed.

5 Undo the elasticated belt and lay it face up on your work surface. Mark the belt with chalk or pins 3 in. (7.5 cm) away from the center front on each side and cut the belt at these points.

6 Measure the depth of the belt and mark this measurement on each side seam, above the hemline. Unpick these sections of the side seams.

7 Insert one section of belt into each side-seam gap, between the front and back of the top; the cut ends of the belt should align with the side seam. Pin in place. Pin one end of each neck tie into each side-seam gap, with the long ends facing outwards. Zigzag stitch the seams back together. Zigzag the raw seam allowances separately. Turn the top right side out. When you put the top on, tie the ties together inside the top and do up the belt at the front to give a nice, nipped-in waist.

8 Hem the bottom of the top with a zigzag stitch (see page 109) and press.

Why not use the excess fabric from the sleeve to make ruffled cuffs? They are particularly useful for ladies with long arms, as they can create a bit of extra length if your sleeves are simply not long enough. You can also turn them around to make it look as if they are attached to your gloves. Depending on how long you want your cuffs to be, you will probably only need one sleeve for this project.

YOU WILL NEED
- Excess sleeve fabric from dress
- 40 in. (1 m) shirring elastic
- Matching thread and sewing needle

1 Cut along the underarm seam and open the sleeve out flat. Decide how long you want your cuffs to be; I made mine 3 in. (7.5 cm) long, plus ¾ in. (2 cm) for the hems. Measure the circumference of your wrist and add ¾ in. (2 cm) for the seam allowance. Cut two rectangles of fabric to these measurements.

2 Using tailor's chalk, mark a line on the wrong side of the fabric, ⅜ in. (1 cm) from the long top and bottom edges for the hem.

STEP 3

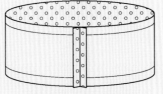

Machine stitch into a loop

STEP 7

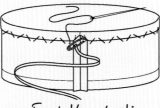

Feed the elastic through the channel

3 With right sides together, taking a ⅜-in. (1-cm) seam, machine stitch the short ends of each rectangle together to form a loop. Press the seam open.

4 Along the long bottom edge of each loop, roll the fabric under to meet the chalked line, pin, then slipstitch in place (see page 109). Press the hem.

5 Repeat step 4 along the bottom edge of the loops, this time leaving a 1-in. (2.5-cm) gap.

6 Wrap elastic around your wrist, pulling it so that it fits snugly but there is still enough stretch for it to go over your hand. Cut two pieces of elastic to this length.

7 Thread the elastic through the casings in the top edge of each loop (see page 122), then secure the elastic in place at each end by overstitchign by hand until you feel it is strong enough. Slipstitch the gap closed.

8 Turn the cuffs right side out.

I find smock dresses easy to source from thrift stores, but only a few body shapes suit this empire-line style—so why not give it an uplift by changing it into a tulip-shaped top?

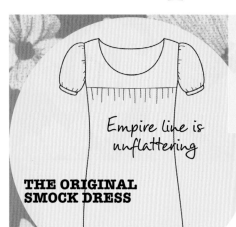

Empire line is unflattering

THE ORIGINAL SMOCK DRESS

A smock dress is useful for maternity wear, but how about giving it a post-pregnancy breath of fresh air by raising the hemline?

YOU WILL NEED
• Empire-line smock dress with capped sleeves
• 1 yd (1 m) bias binding or antique crochet trim, ½ in. (12 mm) wide, for the armholes
• 1¾ yd (1.5 m) antique crochet trim, ⅜ in. (1 cm) wide, for the pocket trim
• Buttons (optional)
• 1 yd (1 m) elastic, ¾ in. (2 cm) wide, for the hem

Take ⅝-in. (1.5-cm) seam allowances throughout unless otherwise stated.

1 Using two tailor's tacks, mark the sleeve and shoulder line to show where the sleeve meets the shoulder seam (see page 113). This will be the point from which you work when constructing the pocket. Staystitch (see page 110) around the sleeves to keep the gathers in place, stitching ⅜ in. (1 cm) down from the seam line.

2 Remove the sleeves by unpicking the armhole seams, making sure the gather stitching stays intact.

3 Bind the armholes with bias binding tape (see page 119) or hem the armholes and sew lace trim into the wrong side, leaving ¼ in. (6 mm) showing.

4 Turn the dress wrong side out and lay it flat on your work surface. Using tailor's chalk, mark all around your desired hemline, then mark another line 2 in. (5 cm) below the first. Cut off the hem along the second line. Fold up and press along the first line, folding under ¼ in. (6 mm) at the top. Machine stitch the hem in place, stitching as close to the edge as possible and leaving a 2-in. (5-cm) gap at one side seam. Turn the top right side out.

5 Try the top on and work out how big you want your pocket(s) to be and where you want to position them. (I opted for only one pocket.) Insert pins to mark the top, bottom, and sides. Take the top off and lay it flat again, with the front facing up, then mark the pocket position with tailor's chalk.

6 Unpick the underarm seam of one of the cut-off sleeves so that you can use the fabric as a pocket and lay it flat on your work surface. Divide the width of your pocket in two, then measure this distance out from each side of the tailor's tack that you made in step 1, add ¼ in. (6 mm) to each side for the pocket side hems, and cut off the excess fabric.

7 Measuring from the raw (cut) edge to the hemmed edge of the sleeve, measure and mark the depth of pocket that you require, add ½ in. (12 mm), and cut off any excess. Fold under ¼ in. (6 mm) at each side and press. Cut a piece of crochet trim the width of the pocket, pin it to the right side of the pocket top, and stitch in place. Along the bottom edge of the pocket, fold under and press

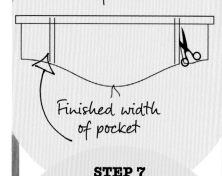

STEP 6
Center of sleeve head

Finished width of pocket

STEP 7
Add crochet trim

Make the pocket

Baste all the way around

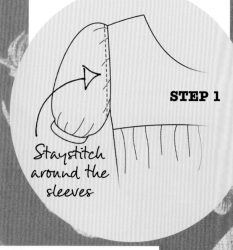

Staystitch around the sleeves

STEP 1

¼ in. (6 mm) twice. Pin the pocket to the top, aligning it with the chalk lines, then baste (tack) it in place.

8 Topstitch the pocket in place, stitching as close to the edge as possible. The gathers from the capped sleeves are already sewn for you! Cut 16 in. (40 cm) of crochet trim, tie it in a bow, and stitch to the center front of the bustline. If you wish, sew buttons to the center front.

9 Thread the elastic through the gap in the hemline (see page 122). Pin both ends together ¼ in. (6 mm) from the ends, with the raw ends facing inward. Machine stitch the two ends together, using a narrow zigzag stitch. Machine stitch the gap in the hemline closed, then gather the hem evenly around the elastic.

STEP 9

Feed the elastic through the hemline

Pretty in pink dress and blouse

Transform your 1980s prom dress into a '50s-style outfit that can be worn in five different ways: as a dress, as a blouse with the buttons at the center front or center back, and with the blouse on top of the dress with the buttons at the center front or center back.

Level
2 Net blouse

The polka-dot pink net had a beautiful array of pearl-effect buttons with fabric loops on the back, providing an Edwardian-style bodice. The sleeves had a mock ribbon tie at each inner cuff. I removed these as I thought they made the blouse look cheap and dated.

YOU WILL NEED
• **One dress with a net overlay, preferably with pearl-effect buttons and loops at the center back**
• **40 in. (1 m) lace, 2 in. (5 cm) wide, with holes suitable for lacing, preferably with a bit of stretch**
• **Approx. 60 in. (1.5 m) ribbon, ¼ in. (6 mm) wide, to tighten lace waistband**
• **Three heart-shaped feature buttons, approx. ½ in. (12 mm) in diameter**
• **40 in. (1 m) pom-pom trim with a little stretch**
• **40 in. (1 m) polka-dot ribbon, ⅜ in. (1 cm) wide**
• **Top or dress with an open neckline**
• **Old dress, top, or bra with adjustable straps**
• **Sparkly elasticated belt (optional)**

Take ⅝-in. (1.5-cm) seam allowances throughout, unless otherwise stated.

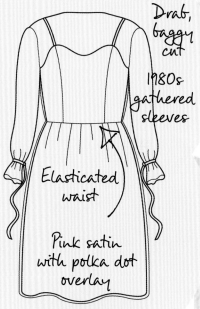

Drab, baggy cut

1980s gathered sleeves

Elasticated waist

Pink satin with polka dot overlay

THE ORIGINAL DRESS

Lace: The amount depends on your waist measurement. The amount given here is based on a dress in US size 6 (UK size 10).

1 Using small scissors, remove the net top section of the dress, cutting above the waistband as close to the seam as possible. Lay the net blouse flat, with the front facing upward, to check that the waistline has nice, clean lines and equal side measurements.

2 Turn the blouse wrong side out. Starting from the center back and leaving ¼ in. (6 mm) overhanging at each end, pin the wrong side of the top edge of the lace to the right side of the net blouse hemline, covering up the raw edges. Zigzag stitch along the top of the lace, folding under the overhanging ends twice to create a neat edge.

3 Pin a small safety pin to the end of the ¼-in. (6-mm) ribbon. Starting at the center back and working from the back through to the front, thread the ribbon in and out of the lace at 1-in. (2.5-cm) intervals. The ribbon will serve as an adjustable waistband for the blouse.

4 Turn the blouse right side out again. Fold under the ends of the ribbon and, using doubled thread, hand stitch heart-shaped buttons onto the ends of the ribbon.

5 Using a small pair of scissors, remove the wrist ribbons (which, in this instance, are purely decorative). On the right side of

STEP 3
Make adjustable blouse waistband

Thread ribbon in and out of lace holes

the blouse, fold under the edge of the pom-pom trim and pin in place. Zigzag stitch the pom-pom trim in place while gently pulling the elastic of the cuff at the same time. When you reach the end of the trim, fold it under so that it meets the other folded-under end neatly and zigzag over these edges to create a neat, flat finish. Repeat on the other sleeve.

6 There is a section of the blouse that requires a finished edge below the Edwardian-style buttons. Pin, baste (tack), and stitch a length of ⅜-in. (10cm) pink polka-dot ribbon over this raw edge to finish it.

7 The original neckline needs to be lowered, as it is too high to be able to wear the blouse both ways. The easiest way to do this is to insert another top or dress with a more suitable neckline underneath the net top and use it as a template. Lay both tops flat on the table and pin them together, then mark the new shoulder seam with tailor's chalk to ensure that they match. Baste (tack) this new neckline, using a contrasting thread. Make sure that the neckline is even all the way around.

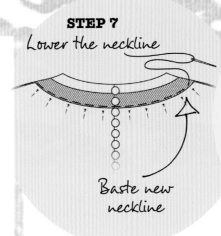

STEP 7
Lower the neckline
Baste new neckline

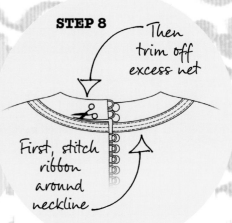

STEP 8
Then trim off excess net
First, stitch ribbon around neckline

8 Starting at the neck opening, baste (tack) a length of ⅜-in. (1-cm) pink polka-dot ribbon over your basting (tacking) stitches, folding the ends of the ribbon under. Stitch along the center of the ribbon, all around the neckline, then repeat along the top and bottom edges of the ribbon. Trim away the excess net from the neckline.

9 Remove the top button and replace it with a sparkly new one to act as a focal point for your blouse.

STYLIST'S TIP
You can wear these this blouse and dress with so many staple items from your wardrobe—combine the net blouse with jeans or the dress with a vintage cardigan, for example.

Level 2 Foundation dress

The satin dress will serve as a foundation garment for the blouse/dress combination. On its own, it needs a bit of updating.

1 Put the dress on and ask a friend to pin the satin skirt to the length you want. Turn the dress inside out. Using tailor's chalk, mark two lines—one where you want the hem to end and another ¾ in. (2 cm) below it. Cut along the lower line. Fold under a narrow double hem (see page 109) along the upper line. Pin, press, and stitch as close to the edge as possible.

STYLIST'S TIP
The idea is that the net skirt overlay should be longer than the satin skirt. The more you raise the hem, the more the skirt will flare out.

2 Unpick the shoulder straps at the seams. Cut the adjustable straps off the old top or bra, just below the attachment seam line. Turn the dress wrong side out. Insert the adjustable straps into the open seams. Pin, baste (tack), and machine stitch them in place.

3 Lift up the bodice facing, then machine stitch the straps securely in place.

4 Turn the dress right side out again. Pin, then machine stitch pom-pom trim between the two front straps of the dress at the top of the bodice, then zigzag stitch as close to the edge as possible.

5 The original dress had two net belt straps, which I secured back to the bodice after I had removed the blouse from it. I then threaded through a sparkly belt: after all, the more fitted the waist, the more the skirt flares out!

Chapter 3
Reconstructing

Reconstructing is to do with recreating the shape of the garment. In this chapter, you will learn to identify the pieces that are worth cutting up and putting back together again, or combining with another item. You may have found a small piece of gorgeous vintage fabric: why not stitch together panels to make a cape (see page 104)? Or you may want to cut up a garment and make it into something else, because part of the fabric is worn or torn: see the Sunshine Dress on page 100, where I combined it with a foundation dress in order to achieve the look that I wanted. As always, the possibilities are endless—so deconstruct, reconstruct, and stitch your way into a whole new look!

1940s-inspired silk blouse

This is a classic, must-have piece for your wardrobe. For a glamorous, 1940s Hollywood look, wear it with some tailored, wide-legged pants and bright red lipstick.

It was the tailored, yet feminine, look of this blouse that made me think it was possible to give it a 1940s feel. I replaced the sleeves on the original blouse as I knew it would lend itself to a full, sheer sleeve.

YOU WILL NEED
• Tailored silk, silk-look, or satin blouse
• Crocheted doily or piece of crocheted fabric that coordinates with the color of the blouse
• Blouse with sheer sleeves (the armhole should be the same size or larger than that of the foundation blouse)
• Vintage buttons that fit the original buttonholes (optional)

Take ⅝-in. (1.5-cm) seam allowances throughout, unless otherwise stated.

1 Place the buttoned-up silk blouse on a table, front facing up, and decide where you want to position the doily. Pin the doily to the blouse, making sure that the pins do not go over the edge of the doily, as they will leaves holes in the fabric.

2 Baste (tack) the doily in place about ¼ in. (6 mm) in from the edge. Machine zigzag stitch as close to the edge of the doily as possible. Straight stitch another line parallel to the first, ¼ in. (6 mm) inside this stitching line.

3 Turn the blouse wrong side out. Using the smallest pair of fabric scissors that you have, carefully cut away the blouse fabric from behind the doily. Turn the blouse right side out again and check that you are happy with the look.

4 Cut off the sleeves of the silk blouse. I cut just below the armhole seam, allowing the tiny seam to fray—a useful technique if you do not feel confident about installing a sleeve!

5 Using tailor's chalk, mark the point where the shoulder seam meets the sleeve on the wrong side of the sheer sleeve, then work a tailor's tack at this point. Cutting below the armhole seam, remove the sleeves from the sheer-sleeved blouse, keeping a note of which is the left and which is the right sleeve.

6. Starting and finishing at the underam seam, measure all around the sleeve heads of both the foundation blouse and the sheer-sleeved blouse. If the sheer sleeve armholes are the same size as those of the foundation blouse, insert the sleeves following the instructions on page 122.

7 If the sheer sleeve armholes are bigger than those of the foundation blouse, work out the difference. Halve the armhole difference measurement and mark this with chalk on either side of the first marked point on the sleeve head. Gather this area by hand (see page 117).

Collar and neckline look dated

THE ORIGINAL BLOUSE

Too tailored and formal

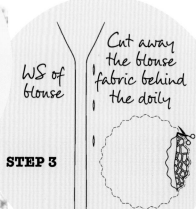

WS of blouse

Cut away the blouse fabric behind the doily

STEP 3

Gather between these marks

STEP 7

8 **With right sides together, pin the sheer sleeves** into the armholes of the foundation blouse, easing them into place (see page 123). Pin in place on the wrong side, within the seam allowance; if you pin outside the seam allowance, it will leave holes in the fabric.

9 **Turn the sleeves right side out** and check that you are happy with the look and that the sleeves are even on both sides. Re-pin the sleeves if necessary.

10 **Turn the blouse wrong side out again.** Starting and finishing at the point where the underarm seam of the sleeve meets the bodice side seam, machine stitch the sleeves in place (see page 123). I then worked another line of stitching ⅟₁₆ in. (2 mm) away from the first, as the sheer fabric was so fragile.

11 **Zigzag stitch the seam** allowance to prevent it from fraying. Turn the blouse right side out.

STYLIST'S TIP
If you wish, change the buttons for an even more vintage look.

DESIGNER TIP To make this blouse look even more 1940s, why not sew in some shoulder pads or add some velveteen ribbon to the side seams to tie at the back for a nipped-in waist?

Prairie dress

Level 3

Want to add a bit of "oomph" to an old, yet faithful, dress? Give it some shape by adding a ruched underskirt.

Ruching is a really easy and effective way of customizing an old dress, skirt, or top! I chose this dress because I liked its mix of autumnal colors. The customizing has given it a sense of movement and it is now much more wearable on a day-to-day basis. The underskirt is a gathered skirt from a high-street store. It has a slight shine, which I felt complemented the matt fabric of the dress.

YOU WILL NEED
- Floor-length dress with a waistline seam, preferably with a zipper at the center back or side seam
- Replacement buttons for center front panel and epaulettes (optional)
- Underskirt, preferably elasticated
- 2 yd (2 m) bias binding for neckline or cotton tape
- 18-in. (45-cm) zipper, if the dress does not already have one
- Co-ordinating fabric for sleeve epaulettes (optional)

Take ⅝-in. (1.5-cm) seam allowances throughout, unless otherwise stated.

1 Put on the dress and stand with your shoulders back in front of a full-length mirror. Work out how long you want the dress to be once ruched. Pin the length (just pin, take the dress off, pin the hem up, and put the dress back on). Then do the same with the sleeves. (You only need to pin one sleeve in order to get an idea of what length you want.) If the dress does not already have a zipper, decide where you want the zipper to go and mark the position with tailor's chalk.

2 Replace the center front buttons (optional). I used mismatched ones to add to the charm.

3 Pin the neckline to the depth that you want. Take the dress off and lay it down flat. Using tailor's chalk, "draw" the shape of the neckline that you want; alternatively, baste (tack) the line with a bright-colored thread.

4 Turn both the underskirt and dress wrong side out and pull the underskirt over the dress. If the underskirt is elasticated, remove the elastic through the underskirt

side seam and pin the waistband of the underskirt to the seam allowance of the dress waistband. If the underskirt has a set (faced) waistband, then line the zipper of the underskirt up with the zipper of the dress and pin the two layers together around the waistband. Straight stitch the underskirt to the seam allowance of the dress waistband, then zigzag stitch each side of the seam allowance separately. If the underskirt is larger than the dress waistband, gather it slightly (see page 117), making sure that the gathers are evenly spaced all the way around.

5 If your dress does not already have a zipper, unpick the side seams of both the dress and the underskirt from the underarm seam on the dress down to the point on both layers at which the zipper will end. Machine stitch each side of the seam allowance separately.

Tight sleeves look old fashioned

Drawstring waist is very 1970!

THE ORIGINAL DRESS

STEP 4
Pull underskirt over the dress

WS of dress

6 Turn the dress right side out.
If you are happy with your new chalked or basted (tacked) neckline, then draw it accurately. You can draw around a large plate if the shape of the neckline lends itself to this; alternatively, make a curved shape for one half of the neckline out of paper, fold the dress in half along the center front, place the paper on the neckline with a piece of dressmaker's carbon paper underneath, and go around the edge with a tracing wheel to be sure that both sides are symmetrical. If you've made your new neckline wider than the original, you will also need to adjust the back neckline to match.

7 Draw a generous seam allowance of 1 in. (2.5 cm). Stay stitch ¼ in. (6 mm) above the chalked or basted neckline to prevent fraying, then cut along the neckline. Face or bind the neckline (see pages 118 and 119). On this dress, I removed the original lace and replaced it on the new neckline.

SEWING TIP
Finish off the edge of the neckline with cotton tape if you don't feel confident about attaching binding.

8 In step 1, you pinned the hem to the length you want the dress to be when ruched. Compare this measurement with the original length of the dress to see how much you need to gather. Pick three evenly spaced points on the center front of the skirt section of the dress at which you are going to create the ruched effect and mark each one with a pin. Divide the total amount that you want to gather by three and gather the skirt by this amount at each marked point by working two parallel rows of large running stitches by hand (see page 117). Put the dress on again to check that it is ruched to the right length, then secure the ruching with machine straight stitches,

STEP 8

Pull threads to ruche the fabric

RS of dress

Work 2 rows of running stitch at each marked point

reverse stitching at the start and finish. Remove the hand gathering stitches.

9 If you want to shorten the sleeves, pin, cut, and hem each one. I also added 1½ in. (4 cm) to the finished sleeve measurement, turned up the sleeves by this amount after hemming to create a turn-up, and topstitched the turn-ups in place.

10 Lay the dress flat and decide how long you want the epaulettes to be. Cut two strips of fabric to the required length and twice the finished width plus a ⅜-in. (1-cm) seam allowance. With right sides together, taking a ⅜-in. (1-cm) seam, machine stitch, then turn the epaulettes right side out. Press flat, with the seam in the center of one side. Topstitch all around, then attach the epaulettes to the shoulders of the dress by stitching across the short ends. I also added a button to each epaulette for decorative purposes.

SEWING TIP
I made the epaulettes out of some sample fabric that I had, but you could use the fabric that you cut off the sleeves.

11 Insert the concealed zipper (see page 124), if your dress does not already have one.

STYLING TIP
This is a good all year-round number. During the colder months, wear it with a cozy cardigan and boots. Dress it up for a wedding or wear it in the summer with flip sandals.

Hot pants

This is a really glitzy project! I managed to get hold of a pair of 1950s pants with the mid-cut shape I was looking for and made my own pattern from them.

This project is more advanced than most of the others in this book. It uses a two-part pattern, comprising the shorts cut as a pair and the gusset piece, as opposed to the usual four-part pattern. I have adapted the pattern so that there are no side seams to ruin the smooth finish and fit.

You can buy sequinned jersey fabric from specialist fabric stores (see Suppliers, page 127). You will need a ballpoint needle on your sewing machine for this project, as it uses stretch fabrics.

YOU WILL NEED
• 2 Hot Pants pattern pieces from pull-out sheet
• 20 in. (50 cm) flat sequinned jersey fabric (for US size 6/UK size 10)
• 8 in. (20 cm) matching spandex/swimsuit fabric for the waistband
• 1 yd (1 m) elastic, ¼ in. (5 mm) wide
• Two 16-in. (40-cm) lengths of ribbon, ⅜ in. (1 cm) wide, for hanging loops
• Ballpoint machine needles
• Matching thread

Take ¾-in. (2-cm) seam allowances throughout, unless otherwise stated.

1 Pin the pattern pieces to the sequinned fabric, following the grain lines marked on the pattern. Cut out two hot pants sides and one gusset piece.

2 With right sides together, matching the notches, pin and baste (tack) the two sides of the hot pants together. Using a ballpoint needle and a narrow zigzag stitch, machine stitch the center front and center back seams. Press the seams flat.

3 On each side of the sequinned fabric, there will be a section of jersey fabric that is free of sequins. Following the grain, cut a strip ¾ in. (2 cm) wide from this fabric and bind (see page 119) the center front and center back seams—fold both sides under and pin, then, using a ballpoint needle and a narrow zigzag stitch, machine stitch the binding in place. Press the bound seams to one side.

4 With right sides together, matching the notches, pin and baste (tack) the gusset between the two sides of the pants. Using a ballpoint needle and a narrow zigzag stitch, machine stitch the gusset in place. Bind the seams, as in step 3.

5 Cut a length of elastic about ¾ in. (2 cm) shorter than the waist of the hot pants, plus a little extra for an overlap. Pin the elastic to one side of the waistband, then stretch it out across the front of the pants so that the halfway point on the elastic meets the other side of the waistband. Pin again, then stretch the remaining elastic around the back of the pants and pin. Pull the elastic very slightly, then machine stitch, using a narrow zigzag stitch.

6 Measure the waist and cut a strip 1 in. (2.5 cm) longer than this and 2 in. (5 cm) wide across the more visible weave of the spandex fabric; when it is cut in this way, spandex has a little less stretch and is easier to sew.

7 Cut two 16-in. (40-cm) lengths of ribbon for the hanging loops. Fold each one in half lengthwise and pin in place on the wrong side of the pants, at the sides.

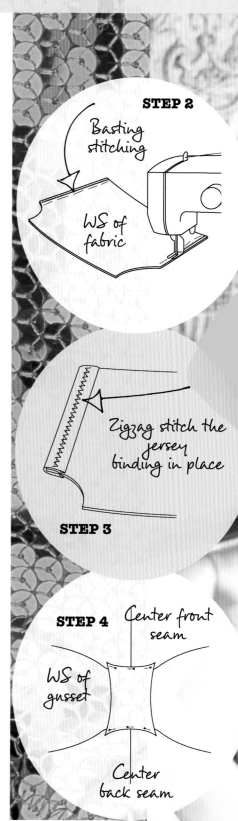

STEP 2
Basting stitching
WS of fabric

Zigzag stitch the jersey binding in place
STEP 3

STEP 4
Center front seam
WS of gusset
Center back seam

STEP 8

Roll the raw edge of the spandex under

8 **With right sides together, pin the spandex strip to the pants,** just under the elastic. Taking a ⅜-in. (1-cm seam), machine stitch the spandex in place, using a narrow zigzag stitch and overlapping the ends of the spandex at the back of the garment. Trim off any excess sequinned fabric at the top of the pants for smoothness and turn the spandex waistband to the inside. Roll the raw edge of the spandex under and pin in place from the outside. Straight stitch the spandex in place, stitching close to the first line of stitching.

9 **Turn up a ¾-in. (2-cm) hem on the legs** of the hot pants and press. Pin and machine stitch from the inside, using a wide zigzag stitch to cover any rough edges. Press firmly, using steam around the back hem to ease in any areas that may have stretched during stitching.

Turn up hem and zigzag stitch from inside

Waistcoat dress

A waistcoat is the most versatile item you can have in your wardrobe—and here's how to extend it into a dress! Grab some of that fabric you've been storing and team it with your waistcoat to make a stunning dress that will stand out in any crowd!

The amount of fabric that you need for the skirt part of this dress will depend on how long you want the skirt to be. I used about 1 yd (1 m) of each of six fabrics. I also found some antique trim, which brings the colors together nicely and borders the hemline in a neat way.

YOU WILL NEED
- Lined waistcoat
- 2 yd (2 m) heavyweight muslin (calico)
- Three to eight co-ordinating fabrics for the skirt section
- Lengths of lace or crochet trim (optional) for the hemline edging
- 12–16-in. (30–45-cm) concealed or heavy-duty zipper
- 10 in. (25 cm) soft coordinating leather
- Decorative items for the lapel (I used vintage buttons and the feather from a fascinator)
- 2 yd (2 m) pattern paper
- Tailor's chalk
- Pencil
- Right angle
- PVA glue

Take ⅝-in. (1.5-cm) seam allowances throughout, unless otherwise stated.

1 First, decide how long you want the dress to be. You could design it as a maxi dress or have the dress shorter than the one in the photo. It is up to you! Work out how you want the dress to look: do you want it to be straight or to have a little flare? If you want a maxi dress, remember to include a split at the center back so that you can walk in it.

2 Button up the waistcoat and topstitch the waistcoat together at the end of the front panel. Remove the existing buttons. Sew the buttons back on (or replace them with different buttons if you wish), stitching through all the front layers of the waistcoat.

3 Now take measurements so that you can make a paper pattern for the skirt section. Lay the waistcoat down flat and measure accurately around the waist. Using tailor's chalk, mark the waistline on the wrong side of the waistcoat, so that you can use it as a guide when you come to position the skirt section. Measure the distance from the waistline to the waistcoat hem.

4 Put the waistcoat on a mannequin, measure down from the waistline to where you want the hem of the skirt to be; make a note of this measurement. (If you do not have a mannequin, put the waistcoat on and stand upright in front of a mirror, with your back straight; hold a tape measure down or ask a friend to measure it for you.)

5 On pattern paper, make a mark to indicate the center front of the skirt. Draw a line down from this point to where you want the hem to finish.

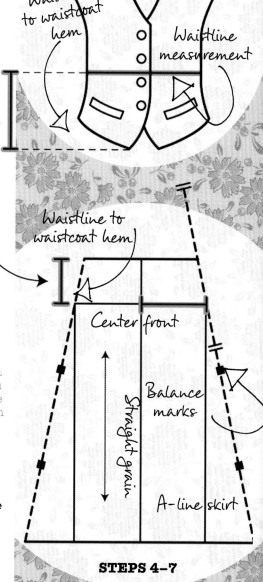

STEP 4

Waistline to waistcoat hem

Waistline measurement

Waistline to waistcoat hem

Center front

Balance marks

Straight grain

A-line skirt

STEPS 4–7

6 **Measure one-quarter of the waist measurement** out from each side of the center point and make a mark at these points. Draw around these points and add notches on either side to ensure balanced seams. Using a ruler and a set square, join up the marks to make a rectangle. If you want a flared A-line, rather than a straight skirt, extend the hem line on the pattern by the required amount, then draw a line (shown by a dotted line on the sketch on page 82) from this point up to the waistline. Add your balance notches to the side seams of the skirt.

7 **Mark where you want the zipper to go.** I inserted the zipper in the right side seam of the dress for a left-handed person to work easily, beginning at the top of the waistcoat underarm side seam.

8 **Add a ⁵⁄₈-in. (1.5-cm) seam** allowance all around, then cut out the paper pattern.

9 **Pin the pattern to the muslin** (calico). Cut two pieces—one for the front and one for the back. Transfer the balance and zipper marks from the pattern to the fabric.

10 **Choose between three and eight different fabrics for the skirt** (I used six fabrics). Using tailor's chalk, mark out strips 2½ in. (6 cm) wide. Following the markings, rip the fabric into strips; I find that the raw edges of these strips add to the earthy look of the dress. I also used strips of lace and tweed to combine feminine and masculine fabrics.

11 **Iron each strip of fabric flat.** At the top of the muslin (calico), measure and mark the distance from the waistline to the waistcoat hem, plus the ⅝-in. (1.5-cm) seam allowance, then start pinning the strips in place, inserting a pin at the top, middle, and bottom of each strip. Leave a space half the depth of the antique trim for the panel at the bottom of the muslin (calico). Check in the mirror that you are happy with how it looks.

12 **Working from the center front strip outward,** top to bottom, machine straight stitch down each strip. You can either straight stitch down the center of each strip or zigzag stitch down each side.

13 **With right sides together, aligning the balance marks,** machine stitch the front and back skirt panels together,

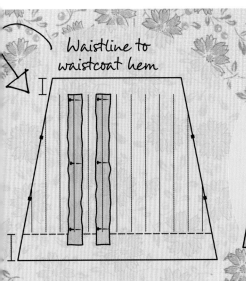

Waistline to waistcoat hem

STEP 11

Leave open for zipper

STEP 13

Fold over

Apply glue

Snip the corners

STEP 15

remembering to leave the side seam open where the zipper is going to go. Press the seams (including the zipper section) open. Overlock or zigzag stitch the seams (see page 115) to prevent the muslin (calico) from fraying.

14 Turn the skirt right side out. Hem the skirt (see page 109). Pin your chosen fabric strip(s) or trim to the hem of the skirt and machine stitch in place.

15 I added leather to the welt pockets of the waistcoat to balance out the colors of the dress. First, measure the welt pocket and add ⅝ in. (1.5 cm) all around for the seam allowance. Cut a piece of leather to this size for each pocket. Snip diagonally into the corners of the leather, up to the end of the seam allowance. Spread a thin layer of PVA glue evenly over the seam allowance and the area onto which the seam allowance will be folded and leave until touch dry. Fold the seam

allowances over to the wrong side, press down, and leave overnight for the glue to dry.

16 Carefully unpick the side seams of the welt pockets. Pin the leather along the top of each pocket. Topstitch all the way around the leather and slipstitch the side seams of the welt pockets back together.

17 Turn the dress wrong side out and trim the skirt hemline. Zigzag stitch or overlock the seam between the skirt and the waistcoat.

18 Turn the dress right side out and unpick the right side seam of the waistcoat section up to the point where the zipper will end. Insert the zipper (see page 125).

19 Add whatever detail you wish to the neckline of the dress. I joined some of the strips together, pleated them, and stitched them to the dress by topstitching through the center. I then added a feather decoration to give the dress a Celtic feel.

STEPS 17–18

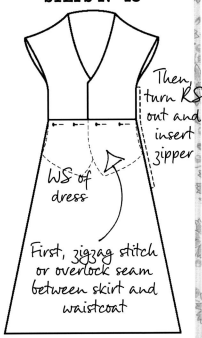

Then, turn RS out and insert zipper

WS of dress

First, zigzag stitch or overlock seam between skirt and waistcoat

DESIGNER TIP
You could insert a zipper that ends at the hem of the dress. This would enable you to open it at the bottom to create a kick flare.

Folklore dress

*Make a new dress from two outgrown ones! This mix-and-match
look is very current in the high-end fashion world.*

Unpick skirt
and waistband

Cut off sleeves
to make
contrast panels

Attach
grosgrain
ribbon to
the dress

Measure length
and cut off
fabric to make
skirt

STEPS 3–5

STEP 6

**What drew me to this
1980s checkered dress
were the leg-of-mutton
sleeves,** so I needed to
include them in the final
look. I happened to have
a 1970s wine-colored polka
dot dress hanging up next
to it, which complemented
the colors and pattern—and
there the idea was born!

Bear in mind that the two
dresses that you use for this
project should be made of
a similar weight of fabric.

YOU WILL NEED
• **Two dresses of a similar weight
of fabric**
• **2 yd (2 m) grosgrain (petersham)
ribbon or cotton tape, 1 in.
(2.5 cm) wide**
• **Iron-on light/medium weight
interfacing to match the weight
of the dress you're using for the
top skirt)—optional**
• **1 yd (1 m) muslin (calico)
—optional**
• **Pattern paper—optional**

Take ⅝-in. (1.5-cm) seam
allowances throughout, unless
otherwise stated.

**1 Decide which dress is going to
provide the main structure** of the
dress: in this instance, it is the
checkered dress. Put it on a
tailor's dummy and decide on
your hem length. If you want to
shorten it, make a note of the
measurement, as you will be
cutting it off at the waist to avoid
having to re-hem the dress.

**2 Decide how much shorter
you want the top skirt** (in this
instance, the polka dot dress)
to be; make a note of the
measurement. Making the top
skirt shorter than the main
skirt adds a little detail to the
hem of the outfit.

**3 Unpick the waistline of the
main dress**, then remove the
waistband and any fastenings—
for example, the zipper or hooks
and eyes. If you want to shorten
the main dress, cut off any
excess fabric at the waist,
remembering to allow for a
⅝-in. (15-cm) seam allowance
at the waist.

**4 Measure the bodice of the main
dress all around at the waist** and
cut a length of soft grosgrain
(petersham) ribbon or cotton
tape to this length, plus 1¼ in.
(3 cm) extra on each side.

**5 Pin the grosgrain (petersham)
ribbon or cotton tape** to the top
of the main dress skirt section,
on the right side, with the raw
ends overhanging the position
of the original fastening.

6 Remove any fastenings from
the second dress. Cut off the skirt
section, adding a ⅝-in. (1.5-cm)
seam allowance at the waist. If
you want the top skirt to be
shorted than the underskirt,
measure up from the hemline
and cut off any excess fabric at
the waist.

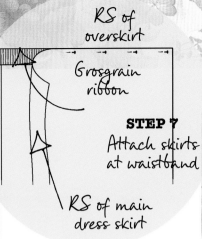

RS of overskirt

Grosgrain ribbon

STEP 7

Attach skirts at waistband

RS of main dress skirt

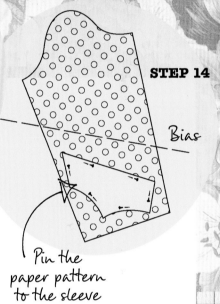

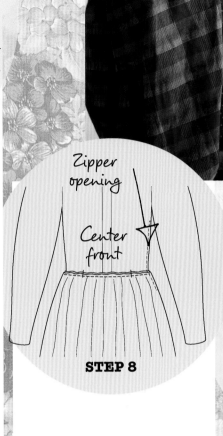

Zipper opening

Center front

STEP 8

STEP 14

Bias

Pin the paper pattern to the sleeve

7 Pin the top skirt over the underskirt at the waist, aligning the raw edges. Check the fullness of the top skirt against that of the underskirt: if your top skirt is fuller, you will need to gather it or pleat it onto the underskirt (see page 117). Try it out on the tailor's dummy as you go to make sure that you are happy with the look. Machine stitch the two skirts together at the waist. Trim the seam allowance of the skirts.

8 With right sides together, aligning the center front, center back, and any zipper openings, machine stitch the bodice to the skirts. Zigzag stitch any seam allowances inside at the waist.

9 Replace the fastenings. If you need a new zipper, decide whether to buy one to match the top skirt or to clash with it for a funky look—but do choose a concealed zipper.

10 Reattach the waistband if there is one (see page 120); in this case, it is attached at the center front and ties in a bow at the back.

11 The final stage—adding contrasting panels from the second dress to the bodice —is optional. It creates the effect of a waistcoat, but it only works if the second dress has large enough sleeves. Cut off the sleeves of the second dress as close to the armhole as you can (unless you want to make a short-sleeved crop top out of the second dress). Cut open the underarm seam as close to the stitching as you can and press the sleeves flat.

12 Using dressmaker's carbon paper and a tracing wheel, trace a panel shape from the bodice of the main dress onto muslin (calico), trying not to go over the bust area too much, especially if you are large busted. Add a ⅝-in. (1.5-cm) seam allowance all around and cut out. Pin the muslin (calico) to the dress and baste (tack) it in place to check that you're happy with the look.

13 If you wish, apply iron-on interfacing to the opened-out sleeves, following the manufacturer's instructions. Use the muslin (calico) that you have just cut out as a template, but remember to remove the seam allowance.

14 Pin the interfaced panels to the opened-out sleeves, either on the straight grain or the bias (see tip below and page 113), and cut out.

SEWING TIP
If the bodice is a snug fit, cut the panels on the bias of the fabric, so that it can stretch over any curves should the pattern of the fabric allow this.

15 Pin the panels right side up on the bodice, then baste (tack) in place. Topstitch in place, then press.

Thermal top with sheer sleeves

Don't hide this chiffon-sleeved thermal top under your clothes—show it off for all the world to see!

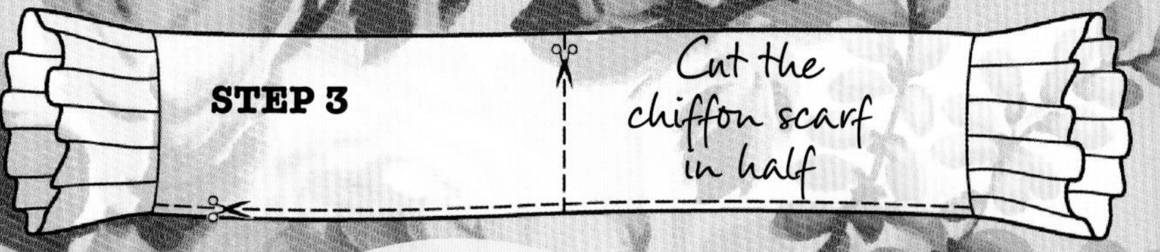

STEP 3

Cut the chiffon scarf in half

THE ORIGINAL THERMAL TOP

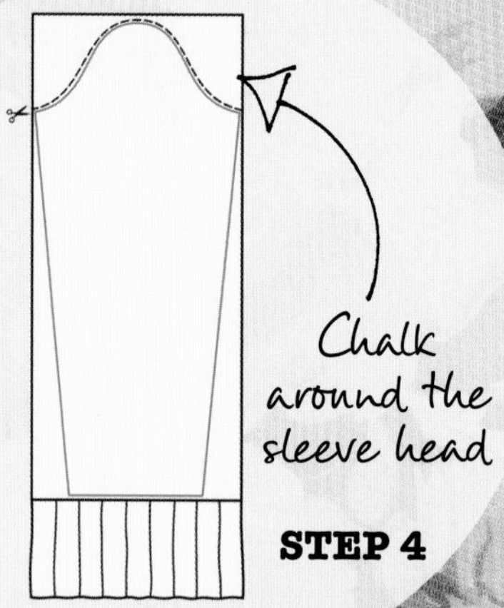

Chalk around the sleeve head

STEP 4

The sleeves were made out of a sheer tubular scarf with embroidered detail. I was drawn to it by its bright colors and stitching. I needed to reflect the bright colors on the thermal bodice, so I stitched some colorful lace and buttons on in order to balance the colors. You could wear this top with a pair of jeans or under a dress.

YOU WILL NEED
• Long-sleeved, plain-colored thermal top
• Double-layered or tubular chiffon or thin sheer scarf
• 2 yd (2 m) stretch lace in two colors
• Button for front detail
• Ballpoint machine needles

Take ⅝-in. (1.5-cm) seam allowances throughout unless otherwise stated.

1 Measure the length of the thermal top sleeves from the top shoulder seam to the cuff and add a ⅝-in. (1.5-cm) seam allowance. This will provide the measurement for your chiffon scarf sleeves.

2 Cut the sleeves off the long-sleeved thermal top as close to the armhole seam as you can, keeping the sleeve head intact. Unpick the long underarm seam of one of the thermal sleeves and open it out.

3 Cut the chiffon scarf in half down the middle so that you have two pieces for the sleeves. If your scarf is tubular, cut along the long seam, too, and open the piece out.

4 On the thermal sleeve, measure down from the sleeve head to where you want your new sleeve to end (see step 1) and mark with tailor's chalk. Aligning this mark with the hemmed end of the tubular scarf, place the opened-out thermal sleeve on one half of the scarf and chalk around the sleeve head. Cut out the chiffon sleeve. You may have a scarf that is too wide, in which case gather it in at the sleeve (see page 117). Repeat on the other half of the chiffon scarf.

5 Insert the sleeves into the thermal top (see page 123), easing in any fullness at the shoulder seams. Using a narrow zigzag stitch and a ballpoint machine needle, machine stitch the sleeves into the armholes.

STEP 6

Trim the seam allowance

Press seam allowance to one side

SEWING TIP
Practice first on off-cuts of the thermal top and sleeve fabric in order to get your stitch tension right, as you have two very different fabrics here!

6 To finish off the armholes, trim the seam allowance, press the seam allowance to one side, and zigzag stitch around the seam from the outside with a matching thread, making sure that you catch the seam allowance in the zigzag stitching so that it doesn't fray.

7 If you are not using a tubular scarf for the sleeves, turn over a double hem at the cuff end of each sleeve and machine stitch.

8 Pin your strips of lace to the wrong side of the neckline, one at a time. Starting at the shoulder seam, stitch them in place with a narrow zigzag stitch, so that it works with the stretch. Sew a decorative button onto the center of the front neck.

Level 4 Patchwork ranch skirt

These instructions are based on the assumption that you have bought a pre-made piece of patchwork and are following a simple A-line skirt or wrap-skirt pattern, although you could make your own pattern from a favorite skirt if you prefer.

Tape one end of each belt loop to raw waist edge

STEP 5

I used an A-line pattern, but I made the skirt look like a wrap skirt by applying a crocheted trim vertically down the front. Why not pair it with a white tank top and a denim jacket for that good old country look?

YOU WILL NEED
- A pre-made piece of patchwork
- A-line or wrap-around skirt pattern with a side zipper
- 40 in. (1 m) thin leather tie or leather shoelaces for the waistband loops
- Approx. 5 ft (1.5 m) vintage trim, 2½ in. (6 cm) wide, for the hemline
- Two 80-in. (2-m) lengths of lace or ribbon with a slight elasticity, up to 2 in. (5 cm) wide
- 80 in. (2 m) crochet trim with a little elasticity, up to 3 in. (7.5 cm) wide
- 8-in. (20-cm) concealed zipper

Take ⅝-in. (1.5-cm) seam allowances throughout, unless otherwise stated.

1 Cut out the paper pattern pieces and pin them to the patchwork. Transfer any markings from the patterns to the fabric, and tailor tack the darts (see page 113).

SEWING TIPS
- For a professional-looking finish, make sure that the squares of the patchwork match up at the side seams of the skirt.
- Place the darts on the seam line of a patchwork square, so that you can ease that dart into the square neatly.

2 Cut out the fabric pieces, then sew the darts (see page 116). (You will need to unpick seams in the patchwork at the relevant points to do this.) Press the darts flat, toward the center back/front of the skirt.

3 With right sides together, machine stitch the panels of the skirt together, remembering to leave 8 in. (20 cm) unstitched at the top of the left side seam for the zipper.

4 Make the waistband (see page 120), using either patchwork or another fabric of your choice.

5 Before you attach the waistband to the skirt, cut eight lengths of leather tie or shoelace, ¾ in. (2 cm) longer than the finished depth of your waistband, for the belt loops. Starting from a side seam, spacing the loops roughly 3–4 in. (8–10 cm) apart, tape one end of each loop to the raw waist edge of the skirt, on the right side of the skirt. Machine stitch in place.

6 With right sides together and pattern markings matching, pin and baste (tack) one long edge of the waistband to the waist edge, sandwiching the leather loops in between, and stitch in place. Fold the other long edge of the waistband and the loops over to the wrong side of the skirt, catching the loops under the waistband edge, then machine stitch in place.

STEP 6

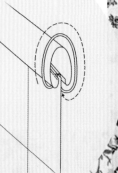

Add the waistband, sandwiching ends of loops between waistband and skirt

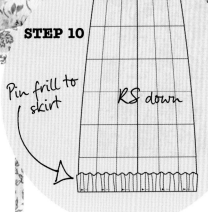

STEP 10 Pin frill to skirt — RS down

STEP 12 Center front — Pin lace, ribbon, and crochet trim along this line

7 From the remaining patchwork (or from a different fabric if you prefer), cut material for the belt. It should be the circumference of your waist plus enough extra to tie the ends and twice the desired final width plus 1⅛ in. (3 cm) for seam allowances. Fold it in half lengthwise, right sides together, and machine stitch along one short edge and the raw long edge. Turn right side out, turn under the short raw ends, and slipstitch closed. Press.

8 Insert the concealed zip at the side seam (see page 125).

9 For the gathered hem, cut a piece of patchwork fabric twice the circumference of the hem and 4 in. (10 cm) deep; you may need to join several pieces together to achieve the right length. Along one long edge, fold under a narrow double hem and press. Machine stitch all the way along. By hand, work two parallel rows of running stitch along the unhemmed long edge and gather to the circumference of the hem, making sure the gathers are evenly spaced.

10 Starting at the side seam, with right sides together, pin the gathered edge of the frill to the bottom of the skirt, making sure the gathers are evenly spaced. Machine stitch, then zigzag stitch each side of the seam allowance separately. Then, working on the right side, stitch on the seam line for a neat, professional finish.

11 Lay the skirt flat, right side facing upward, and pin the vintage trim just above the seam between the skirt and the gathered hem, leaving about ½ in. (12 mm) of each end of the trim overhanging at one side seam. Unpick the same side seam to the depth of the trim and turn the raw ends of the trim to the wrong side. Zigzag stitch along the top of the trim to secure it in place, then turn the skirt inside out and re-stitch the unpicked section of side seam.

12 Turn the skirt right side out again and lay it flat on your work surface, with the front facing upward. Measure halfway from the center front to the side seam on whichever side you want to create the "wrap-around" effect. Following the lines of the patchwork, pin lace/ribbon along this line, from below the waistband to the hem of the skirt. Pin another length of lace

or ribbon halfway over the first, then straight stitch in place, stitching along both edges of the lace or ribbon.

SEWING TIP
Do not pull the crochet while sewing, otherwise the skirt will ride up too high. The elasticity of the ribbon/lace will naturally pull the skirt up slightly.

13 Overlap the crochet trim on the top lace, then zigzag stitch along both sides of the crochet down to the hem. Pin another length of crochet just below the waistband and stitch in place in the same way.

14 Feed the patchwork belt through the leather loops to complete the skirt.

DESIGNER TIP This skirt can be made from an existing piece of patchwork (an old quilt cover would work well) or you can make your own, using either worn cotton clothes or "fat quarters," which you can buy from quilt stores. You can buy fat quarters in coordinating bundles of different designs.

1920s butterfly dress

I decided to replace the drop-waist panel of this 1920s dress with an embellished panel from a separate top to transform it into an evening dress.

Crossover top

Existing embroidered detail can be topstitched

THE ORIGINAL DRESS

Sleeves too tight so fabric is torn

I would never normally suggest cutting up such an old dress, but this one had such narrow sleeves that you could not even put your hand into them and, as a result, the fabric was torn. It also looked rather funereal!

YOU WILL NEED
• Drop-waisted dress
• Top of similar weight with embellished detail
• Matching machine thread
• 1 yd (1 m) bias binding or cotton tape to match color of dress
• Sewing needle

Take ⅝-in. (1.5-cm) seam allowances throughout unless otherwise stated.

1 Lay the dress right side up on your work surface, with the front facing up. Cut the back off the embellished top, as you will only be using the front. Decide where you want the embellished design to sit on the drop-waist panel and pin it in place. I took care to ensure that the art deco-style lines stretching out from the butterfly embellishment aligned with the nip tucks on the bodice.

SEWING TIPS
• The embellished top must be of a similar weight to the dress fabric and not cut on the bias.
• You can apply your own design to the existing panel or alternatively, you can replace the entire drop-waist panel.
• Make sure that the replacement panel is wide enough to cover the original waist panel.
• My embellished top was made of chiffon. Inserting pins into this fabric can leave holes, so I took care to pin over the embroidered detailing.

2 Turn the dress inside out and lay it with the front facing toward you. Sew tailor's tacks or chalk notches on both the dress and the drop-waist panel to use as balance marks later on. Unpick the drop-waist panel of the dress all the way around and put the dress to one side.

3 Place the drop-waist panel on the embellished panel, over the section that you want to cut out. Using tailor's chalk, draw around it. Add a seam allowance all around, and cut out with long-handled dressmaking scissors. Staystitch all around the panel about ¼ in. (6 mm) from the edge to prevent fraying (see page 110).

4 Where you cut off the original waist panel, turn under the raw edges along the seam line and press. Aligning the notches, pin the panel right side down to the wrong side of the dress and baste (tack) in place just below the original seam line. If the fabric is sheer, it is more likely that holes will form when it is pinned, so try to pin where the decoration is, rather than on the chiffon. Turn the dress right side out to check that you are happy with the look.

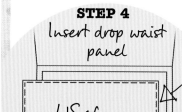

STEP 4
Insert drop waist panel

WS of panel

WS of dress

Baste panel in place

Topstitch over original tuck seams in contrasting thread

Remove sleeves and bind armholes

STEPS 6–7

5 Turn the dress wrong side out again. Using a medium straight stitch and following the original seam lines, stitch the panel in place. Zigzag stitch the raw edges of the seam allowance together to ensure a stronger seam.

6 Turn the dress right side out and work a decorative machine stitch around the panel edge to flatten the seam edge. I also emphasized the art deco-style tucks on the cross-over section of the dress by stitching over the existing lines in a silvery-gray thread.

7 Remove the sleeves just below the armhole seams, with a small, sharp pair of scissors. Starting at the underarm seam, bind the armholes (see page 119) for a professional finish.

Belt strap dress

If your party dress needs a glamorous new look, how about replacing the original straps with a sash-style belt that can be worn in different ways?

Replace straps

THE ORIGINAL DRESS

Add hemline ruffle

STEP 3

WS of dress

Gather by hand and then pin in place

STEP 4

Overstitch belt ring to front neckline

YOU WILL NEED
- **Party dress**
- **40 in. (1 m) light net**
- **Woven belt with two metal ring fastenings, at least 40 in. (1 m) long**
- **Matching machine and buttonhole thread**
- **Ruler/Right angle**

Take ⅝-in. (1.5-cm) seam allowances throughout unless otherwise stated

1 Turn the dress wrong side out and unpick the facing where the straps meet the dress at the front and the back. Unpick the straps and put them to one side to use later. Stitch the facing back in place neatly.

2 For the hemline ruffle, measure the circumference of the hem, then triple this measurement. Decide how deep you want the ruffle to be and add 1¼ in. (3 cm) to allow for the hem and seam allowance. Cut a strip of net to

this measurement (you will need to sew several strips together to achieve the correct length). Hem one long side of the net.

3 Turn the dress wrong side out. Work two rows of long running stitches by hand along the unhemmed edge of the net, then pull the threads to gather the strip to roughly one-third of its original length. Pin the gathered edge of the net to the hemline of the dress and zigzag stitch securely in place.

4 Using buttonhole thread, overstitch one ring of the woven belt to the center of the front neckline facing, ½ in. (12 mm) below the neckline edge. (The other ring hangs on the outside of the dress.)

5 Put the dress on and ask a friend to take the belt over the left shoulder to the back bodice. Where the belt meets the back bodice, make a mark (either with pins or tailor's chalk) on either side of it as a positional guide for the loops.

6 Take the straps that you cut off the dress in step 1. Measure the width of the belt, add ¼ in. (5 mm), and cut two strips from the strap to this length for the belt loops.

7 The first loop will go on the right side of the back of the dress. Pin the right-hand edge of the loop 2½ in. (6 cm) below the first mark that you made in step 5, and machine stitch across it.

STEP 5

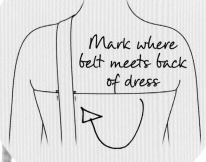

Mark where belt meets back of dress

Add loops made from original dress straps

Fold the loop back on itself and slipstitch the left-hand end in place by hand.

8 Repeat step 7, this time on the wrong side of the back of the dress just 2 in. (5 cm) down from your first marked point. The belt will be fed through this loop first, and then back over the top of the dress and through the loop on the outside of the dress.

9 Feed the belt from the front up through the loop on the inside back of the dress, and then back over the top of the dress and through the loop on the outside of the dress. You can then leave it hanging (the two loops will hold it in place) or you can take it back to the front over the right shoulder. Feed the belt through the back of both metal rings, then take it over the top metal ring and under the bottom metal ring. The loose end of the belt can be pinned—for example, with a brooch—or sewn in place. I prefer to pin it so that I can arrange the belt strap differently each time I wear it.

Level **4** Sunshine dress

I loved the colors of this 1970s handmade smock dress, but felt that it needed a more exciting shape. I used the bodice of a boned, strapless dress as a foundation garment and applied panels of the 1970s dress on top. I also teamed it with a skirt (see page 103) to provide two looks in one.

THE ORIGINAL 1970S DRESS

Gorgeous fabric but lacks shape

THE PURPLE TIERED DRESS

Boned bodice gives shape and structure

Color picks up pink and purple of 1970s dress

YOU WILL NEED
- **Bright-colored vintage dress**
- **Boned strapless dress, preferably with a tiered skirt**
- **Sleeveless top in complementary color**
- **60 in. (1.5 m) fine piping cord**
- **40 in. (1 m) fabric for the piping cut on the bias into strips wide enough to encase the cord plus two seam allowances (1¼ in./3 cm)**

Take ⅝-in. (1.5-cm) seam allowances throughout, unless otherwise stated.

1 **Turn the boned dress inside out** and remove the skirt from the bodice section by unpicking or cutting the seam with small scissors. Remove the side-seam zipper and put the skirt to one side for use later. Remove the boning from the bodice.

2 **Now create a heart-shaped bodice line** to show off more of the T-shirt that will be attached underneath. Using tailor's chalk, draw a heart-shaped line on the wrong side of the bodice front and then staystitch (see page 110) to prevent fraying. Cut along this line, then snip into the curves at regular intervals, so that the fabric will lie flat.

3 **Measure the heart-shaped bodice line all around** and cut a piece of fabric on the bias to this length and wide enough to encase the cord plus 1¼ in. (3 cm) for the seam allowances (see page 119). (You may need to stitch strips together to achieve the right length.)

4 **Fold the bias-cut fabric in half lengthwise,** wrong sides together, with the piping cord in the center, and pin diagonally. Using a zipper foot on your machine, stitch along the length of the fabric as close to the cord as possible. Zigzag stitch the raw edges of the binding together. Put the piping temporarily to one side.

5 **On the right side of the bodice, mark balance points** with tailor's chalk between the bodice sections and number each piece with chalk.

STEP 6

Unpick and number bodice panels

1   2   3

Balance marks

6 **The boned bodice has two layers of fabric.** Separate the top layer from the bottom layer by unpicking it or using a small sharp pair of scissors. Keep the bottom layer intact, and place it to one side. Chalk balance marks between the top layer bodice pieces. Unpick the individual pieces of the top layer from each other. Number each top layer bodice piece, then place them to one side in order.

7 **Cut the 1970s dress along the side seams to separate the front from the back** and remove the straps. Press the pieces flat. Using tailor's chalk, mark grain lines down the fabric at 4-in. (10-cm) intervals so that you can use them as guide lines when you cut out the pattern pieces.

8 **Place the unpicked bodice sections of the boned dress right** side up on your work surface, with tracing paper on top, and

STEP 13

Insert sleeveless top between layers of bodice

Top layer of bodice

RS of bodice

Bottom layer of bodice

13 **Take off the dress and sleeveless top.** Turn the dress wrong side out. Pin the bottom layer of the bodice back in place, sandwiching the top in between the two bodice layers. Restitch along the piping stitching line. Baste (tack) the sleeveless top to the bottom layer of the bodice at both the front and the back of the dress, then cut off the excess sleeveless top.

14 **With right sides together,** matching balance marks, machine stitch the skirt to the bodice around the waistline, leaving the side seam with the zipper unstitched. Finally, insert the zipper (see page 125).

draw around them, adding a ⅝-in. (1.5-cm) seam allowance all around each piece. Draw the fabric grain lines and the balance marks, and number each pattern piece so that you get them in order. Cut out.

9 **Pin the tracing-paper patterns to the 1970s fabric** and cut out. Transfer the balance marks from the pattern pieces to the fabric (see page 113). Place the bodice pieces in order on your work surface.

SEWING TIP

Do you want to match the fabric pattern across adjoining pieces? If so, the best way is to trace the designs onto the tracing paper and then match them together. However, the design of this fabric was so busy that it wasn't obvious that the pattern didn't match perfectly.

10 **Place the 1970s bodice pieces right side up** on the right side of the foundation dress bodice pieces. At this point insert the boning back in place, using a zipper foot when sewing around the boned bodice pieces. Baste (tack) all around, working between the seam lines and the edge of the bodice, then machine stitch just inside the seam line.

11 **With right sides together, matching balance marks,** machine stitch the bodice pieces together in order. Zigzag stitch the seam allowances to prevent fraying, then press the seams open. Snip into the binding to achieve a nice, curved shape.

12 **The sleeveless top goes in between the top and bottom layers of the bodice.** Put the top on, with the dress on top, and ask a friend to insert pins on both the dress and the top at the points where the straps of the top meet the dress.

Level 2 — Sunshine skirt

I decided to make a detachable skirt from a coordinating fabric. It has a fabulous swing to it and can be worn all year round. How about wearing a full net skirt underneath to emphasize that swing in a contrasting color? The larger amounts of fabric given below are in case you want to match pattern repeats across seams or to lengthen the skirt.

YOU WILL NEED
- 6 Sunshine Skirt pattern pieces from pull-out sheet
- 2³/₄–3³/₄ yd (2.5–3.5 m) fabric
- 2¹/₄ yd (2 m) crochet trim, 3 in. (7.5 cm) wide, for the waistline
- 40 in. (1 m) broderie anglaise, 1¹/₂ in. (4 cm) wide, for the hemline
- 20 in. (50 cm) iron-on interfacing to match weight of skirt fabric
- 8-in. (20-cm) concealed zipper
- Hook-and-eye fastening
- 4–6 buttons, approx. ¹/₂ in. (12 mm) in diameter

Take ⁵/₈-in. (1.5-cm) seam allowances throughout unless otherwise stated.

1 Wash, dry, and press the fabric.

2 Trace the pattern pieces you need onto pattern paper, remembering to copy any pattern markings, and cut out. Note that you should take ¾-in. (2-cm) seam allowances along the edges where the zipper will go (as marked on the pattern). Pin the paper patterns to the fabric and cut out, then transfer any pattern markings to the fabric. Remove the pattern pieces, then overlock or zigzag stitch the raw edges of all the fabric pieces and press them again.

3 Following the manufacturer's instructions, apply iron-on interfacing to the wrong side of the waistband facings (see page 120).

4 With right sides together, matching balance marks, pin then machine stitch the skirt panel pieces together, leaving the zipper section unstitched. Press the seams open.

5 Insert the concealed zipper (see page 125).

6 Turn the skirt right side out. Using a regular stitch length and matching thread, stay stitch ⅜ in. (1 cm) from the cut edge all the way around the hemline to prevent fraying and to give an earthy look to the skirt. With right sides together, attach panels to the bottom of the skirt where marked on the pattern. Press the seams open. Following the lines marked on the pattern, pin and zigzag stitch broderie anglaise and crochet trim to the hemline of the skirt.

7 Starting at the side zipper, pin and machine stitch crochet trim to the waistline in the same way.

8 With right sides together, matching balance marks, pin and machine stitch the waistband facings together across one short end.

9 With right sides together, pin, baste (tack), and machine stitch the facing to the top of the skirt. Trim one side of the seam allowance to reduce bulk and zigzag stitch each side of the seam allowance separately.

10 Turn the facing to the wrong side and press along the waist edge. Hand stitch the hem of the facing to the wrong side of the skirt. Do not attach it to the zipper section of the skirt.

11 Turn under the ends of the facing and slip hem to the zipper tape. Attach a hook-and-eye fastening to the top of the zipper. Hand stitch a button to the base of each point on the skirt hemline, ¼ in. (6 mm) up from the base of the point.

reconstructing 103

1970s cape

I love this 1970s fabric. I didn't have enough of it to make a whole cape, so I alternated panels of the '70s fabric with a similar-weight upholstery fabric. The shearling collar was from an existing coat that was a bit worn and had a broken zipper.

STEP 4

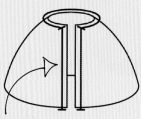

First, measure the length of collar needed

Then, remove required amount of collar from coat

YOU WILL NEED
- 5 1970s Cape pattern pieces from pull-out sheet
- 40 in. (1 m) medium-to-heavyweight fabric
- 40 in. (1 m) coordinating fabric of a similar weight
- 40 in. (1 m) shearling or faux fur fabric
- 18-in. (45-cm) open-ended zipper
- 40 in. (1 m) satin lining fabric
- Frog clasp
- Buttonhole thread to match the cape color

Take ⅝-in. (1.5-cm) seam allowances throughout, unless otherwise stated.

1 Trace the pattern pieces onto pattern paper, transfer any pattern markings, and cut out. Pin the pattern pieces to the fabric and cut out, remembering to transfer any markings to the fabric. Zigzag stitch around each piece to prevent fraying.

2 Matching balance marks, pin and machine stitch the panels of the cape together, then press the seams open.

3 Using a matching thread, topstitch along each side of each seam, stitching ¼ in. (6 mm) away from the seam.

4 Attach the front facing (see page 118), press, and then topstitch ¼ in. (6 mm) away from the center front line.

5 Measure the hemline of the cape and cut a panel to this length and about ½ in. (12 mm) deep from one of the cape fabrics. With right sides together, pin the panel to the hemline of the cape and stitch in place along the bottom edge. Turn the panel to the inside of the cape and press. Turn under the raw edge and slipstitch the top edge of the panel to the inside of the cape.

6 Measure from the hem of the center front of the cape up to the neckline, then all around the neck and back down to the center front hem. Mark out the same measurement on the shearling coat collar, add a ⅝-in. (1.5-cm)

seam allowance along the unzipped edges, then cut out.

7 With right sides together, pin the collar around the neckline of the cape. Starting at the center back, machine stitch the neckline edge of the collar to the cape and then zigzag stitch the seam allowances. Using buttonhole thread, herringbone stitch (see page 109) the free edge of the shearling to the wrong side of the cape.

8 Remove the old zipper from the shearling coat. Pin the new open-ended zipper to the center front of the cape, making sure it extends up to the top of the collar. Baste (tack), then machine stitch in place.

SEWING TIP
Stitch binding to the new zipper before you stitch it in place, as this will help prevent the shearling from stretching.

9 Using the cape pattern pieces, cut out the satin lining. With right sides together, machine stitch the panels together. Press the seams open. Hem the neckline and center front edges of the lining (see page 109).

STEP 7

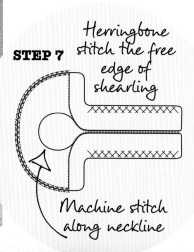

Herringbone stitch the free edge of shearling

Machine stitch along neckline

Slipstitch lining to CF wrong side of cape

10 With wrong sides together, matching balance marks, machine stitch the lining in place along the neckline stitch line. Staystitch (see page 110) around each panel except the facing panel to prevent the fabric from fraying. Slip stitch the lining to the center front of the cape, along the herringbone-stitched edge of the shearling.

11 With the cape right side out, using buttonhole thread, hand stitch the woven frog clasp in place on the center front of the cape.

DESIGNER TIP
Why not use a bright pink or leopard print fabric as the lining for this project? There are many cool linings available now, just crying out to be used in items such as this!

EQUIPMENT

The definitive sewing kit

I am a great believer in starting small when it comes to buying sewing equipment, rather than stocking up on a whole lot of things you might not use. This list is what I think you need to start off with, and when you know that you want to pursue with sewing, you can then invest in more equipment.

Dressmaking shears

Long-handled scissors with bent handles are useful, as they allow the scissors to lie flat on the surface whilst you are cutting. If you look after them, they will last for years and are likely to be the most important investment you can make. Never use them on paper, as this will quickly blunt them.

Small, sharp-ended scissors

These are great for snipping into seams and places that larger scissors cannot reach and also for cutting off stray threads after finishing a seam.

Pinking shears

They can be costly but again are very useful when sewing. They cut fabric leaving a zigzag fray-resistant edge which is useful for seam edges. They are also a great tool for decoration in customizing.

Sewing machine (not shown)

Old sewing machines can be as useful as the new shiny ones. They may not do embroidery motifs at the press of a button—but they do work hard. I have two old sewing machines that I have used for years, including my partner's late grandmother's machine. She was a seamstress and I feel privileged to carry on her sewing legacy!

You can buy a secondhand sewing machine relatively cheaply: you just need time and luck! I found one of mine at my local charity store. Search on local sites, leave messages at charity shops, antique shops, online second-hand sites. We all look for different things when buying a sewing machine. My advice is to attend a class, or have a go on a friend's machine to establish what you need in a machine. Sewing machine stores can provide a wealth of advice, too. The basics I would start with would be the option of different feet (you don't have to buy them all at once if they don't come with the machine), including a zipper foot. It is also useful to have a variety of different stitches that can be used for both functional and decorative purposes, but you don't need to immediately go for the most expensive computer-driven machine.

Machine needles

Buy a range of different needles: you can never have enough of them. Choose a needle that is suitable for the fabric you are using: the lower the number, the finer and thinner the needle. Needles also have different points, each designed for a different type of fabric. The most common are the sharp-point (for woven fabrics) and the ball-point (for knitted fabrics). There are also specialist needles for leather and heavy denim/canvas-type fabrics. You can purchase packets of machine needles with a variety of these needles.

Adjustable dummy

These can be costly when new, but they can save you a lot of time. You can always add batting (wadding) to the form to replicate your size. If you are looking to buy one, then keep an eye out in local papers, online, and at garage sales. If you are not at this stage why not make yourself a dress form of your own? See page 111 for a budget version.

Set square (not shown)

A set square gives true right angles, which is very useful in dressmaking. This is particularly useful for drawing lines at exact right angles and following the bias grain of fabric (see page 113)—for example, if you are making self facing binding.

Thimble

Using a thimble helps you avoid pricking your finger when hand sewing. Try several to find one that is comfortable for you.

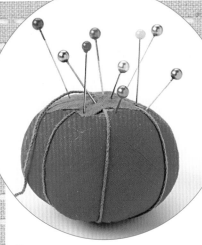

Pins

Pins come in an array of different sizes and lengths to suit different fabric types. For general sewing, glass-headed pins are the easiest to handle. Always have too many and put them in a pincushion to keep them safe and accessible.

Seam ripper

This is used to unpick incorrect stitches and seams quickly—an essential addition to your sewing kit!

Tape measure

This is essential for all sewing jobs: you may think that you can measure by eye, but always check first!

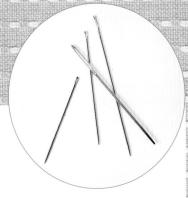

Hand-sewing needles

Hand-sewing needles should be fine enough to slip through fabric but strong enough not to break or bend. Sharps are the needles used most for hand sewing. They are available in a number of sizes from 1 to12; the higher the number, the shorter and finer the needle. A size 9 is the most useful. Try and put the needle through the fabric first to check before sewing as to which one best suits the fabric.

Chalk

Use chalk for transferring pattern markings to fabric and for drawing around pattern pieces. It is available as a pencil or in a wedge called tailor's chalk, which you can easily sharpen with a knife.

Iron (not shown)

A steam iron is indispensable for ironing and pressing open seams. If you do not have a steam iron, use a pressing cloth or a damp muslin cloth. I would always advise to iron on the wrong side of the garment when ironing.

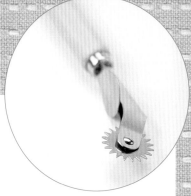

Tracing wheel

This is useful for transferring patterns and their markings from a pattern sheet. However, the metal-pronged wheel may damage the surface of your work table, so you will need to protect it. Dressmaker's carbon paper is a good alternative.

Pattern paper (not shown)

If you want to make your own patterns, you will need suitable paper. Brown parcel paper is suitable, as is tissue paper.

Your work space

Your work area is as important as the tools you work with! A well-organized working area is the first step toward successful designing and making. It must be well lit. If you are able to position your sewing machine with the working end (the needle) of the machine by the window so that there are no shadows, this will help. If you have to work in artificial light, always take a minute to take the item outside, or near a window so that you can check that the colors do indeed work together. When setting up your work space, bear in mind that you will need easy access to electric points and to your sewing equipment.

Sourcing fabrics and trims

My view is that the best place to start when looking for items to revamp or customize is your own wardrobe. Baggy tops can be pulled in with a bit of shirring, an elasticated hem, or waistline. Dated collars can be embellished with sparkly gems or replaced with something a little more fashionable; washed-out colors can be brought up to date with fabric dye or topstitched with a funky contrasting-colored thread.

Secondhand clothes can be so much fun to source and can be bought from thrift stores and garage sales, or acquired as hand-me-downs. If you are short of money or time why not organize a clothes-swapping party with your friends? You can kill two birds with one stone and get some valuable socializing time in with your friends while updating your wardrobe at the same time! I think everyone, with a little encouragement, has their own answers on how to update their own clothes—but who better to talk to about this to than your friends?

Sourcing vintage clothes is becoming increasingly difficult—but wow, what a buzz when you manage to find something special! These days, buying them is more like a competitive sport. They are definitely harder to source but are so special. They were often hand made with great care and attention. To buy pieces of similar quality these days would cost a small fortune to buy (look at current couture prices—they are that level for a reason!). Moreover, all vintage pieces have stories to tell, which is what makes them special. I feel that the most important thing is to not be too precious about them: respect them, but enjoy them and rework them if they need a lift or a bit of TLC. Don't be afraid to cut into them. If it means that you are enjoying them (and others, by you wearing them!) then go for it, girl!

Trims

Adding trims can be one of the quickest and most satisfying aspects of customizing, as they can help add instant individuality and style to your piece of clothing. To think, you can buy a dress on a Saturday afternoon and with a little work you can have your own designer piece to wear that very night! There are some really beautiful trims available these days, both old and new; some are so beautiful that I could easily design an entire look around one piece of lace, for example.

Whether you're trawling through thrift stores or rummaging through bargain buckets at bric-a-brac sales, if you really fall in love with something, snap it up as soon as you see it. You may not immediately know what to do with it—but one day, I promise you, you will find the perfect item to match it with!

In addition to purpose-made trims, don't overlook other items that can be cut up and used for decoration: They can come from all sorts of sources. For example, if I want to give an ultra-feminine silk dress an industrial look, I go to my local chandlery or ironmongers. Even items such as crocheted doilies and hand-embroidered tray cloths can be pressed into service.

Life-altering trims can come in all shapes and sizes: buttons and sequins, ribbons and rick-rack, or fabric samples, beads and bits of broken jewelry: you just need to see the potential in it. Remember, you are the designer! If you feel that you need a little assistance, then hopefully *Fashion Hacks* will be able to guide you.

Get in the mood!

If you need help and inspiration when it comes to customizing a garment to your own style, check out magazines, fashion books, theatre/film costumes, or vintage illustrations, as well as current trends. I am a real fan of 1970s and 1940s style, which I incorporate into my day-to-day style. Why not photocopy or cut out images that you like and put them together in a notebook or on a large sheet of card that you can use as a mood/inspirations board? These are used at fashion college to inspire students with their designs. Even if you don't make direct use of it, you can always stick it up on the wall and enjoy looking at your favorite looks.

TECHNIQUES

Basic stitches

A few simple stitches are all you need to know in order to sew with confidence!

Hand stitches

Although most stitching is done by machine, you will usually need to use some form of hand stitching in the process of creating or customizing a garment. These stitches are useful for temporarily holding pieces of fabric together, sewing up gaps in seams, and for working neat, occasionally invisible hems.

Basting (tacking)
This stitch is used to temporarily hold two or more pieces of fabric together. Working from right to left (reverse this if you are left-handed), take short, evenly spaced stitches about ¼ in. (6 mm) long, stitching close to the seamline but inside the seam allowance. Take several stitches onto your needle at one time before drawing the thread through.

Overhand stitch
This stitch is used to hold two finished edges together. Working from right to left (reverse this if you are left-handed), insert the needle diagonally through the edges, picking up one or two fabric threads from the back and then from the front edge. Draw the thread through. Insert the needle directly behind the thread from the previous stitch and bring it out a little to the left, through the front edge. Continue until the two edges are joined.

Slipstitch
This stitch is used to sew up a seam, or a gap in a seam, quickly and easily from the right side of the fabric. Working from right to left (reverse this if you are left-handed), bring the needle through one folded edge, slip it through the fold of the opposite edge for about ¼ in. (6 mm), and draw the needle and thread through. Continue in this way to join both edges.

Herringbone stitch
This is a strong, flat hemming stitch worked from left to right, with the needle pointing to the left. (Reverse this if you are left-handed.) Bring the needle out through the hem edge. Take a very small backward stitch into the garment directly above the hem edge, ¼–⅜ in. (6–10 mm) to the right. Take the next stitch into the hem, ¼–⅜ in. (6–10 mm) to the right. As you stitch, the threads will cross over themselves.

Flat hemming stitch
This is the quickest of all hand-hemming stitches. Working from right to left (reverse this if you are left-handed), secure the thread on the inside of the hem fabric. Pick up one or two threads of the garment, then bring the needle up through the folded hem edge and pull the thread through.

Blind hemming stitch
Neaten the hem edge and press the hem allowance to the inside. Pin and baste (tack) the hem in place close to the folded hem edge. Work from right to left, with the needle pointing to the left. Take a very small stitch in the garment, then take the next stitch ¼ in. (6 mm) to the left in the hem allowance. Continue until the hem is secured, then remove the basting (tacking) stitches.

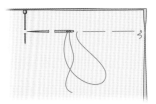

Basting (tacking)

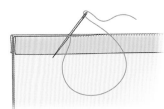

Overhand stitch

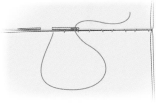

Slipstitch

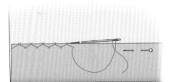

Herringbone stitch

Flat hemming stitch

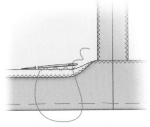

Blind hemming stitch

Machine stitches

The majority of all sewing machines can do straight and zigzag stitches; consult your instruction manual to find out how to alter the length and width of these stitches. The following are machine straight stitches used for specific purposes.

Topstitching

Topstitching adds a crisp, decorative finish and can be done using normal sewing thread, or a heaver topstitching thread (which is more suited to thicker fabrics). Topstitching can be purely decorative, serve a functional purpose, or both. You can use either a matching or a contrasting color of thread and have real fun with it!

Staystitching

Staystitching is a row of machine stitching that is worked on the cut garment pieces before you start to sew them together. It is used on curved and bias seams such as necklines to stop them from stretching while you make up the garment. Work a row of medium-length straight stitches just inside the seam allowance of the cut piece.

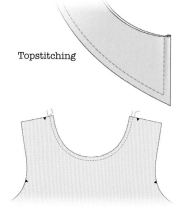

Topstitching

Staystitching

Taking body measurements

Taking measurements may seem a bit tiresome, but if you take the time to do it properly before you begin making or customizing your clothes, you will reap the benefits later.

It is possible to measure yourself, but I strongly advise you to ask a friend to help. For the most accurate results, have your measurements taken in your underwear and remove your shoes. If you are having clothes altered, always take into account the shoes that you have on at the time or the lowest heels that you are likely to wear with the outfit. Tie some string around your waist as a guide. Bear in mind that you will have days when your measurements will fluctuate slightly.

Basic measurements

1 Bust

Measure around the fullest part of the bust. Measure across the widest part of your back, under your arms, and across the fullest part.

2 Waist

Take this measurement comfortably around the waist at the point where your belt sits.

3 Waist to hips

This is the distance from your waist to the widest part of your hips.

4 Hips

This is the fullest part of your hips. Make sure that the tape measure does not slip down while you are measuring.

5 Neck to waist

Measure from the nape of the neck down to the waist at both front and back.

6 Height

Remove your shoes and stand up against a wall. Place a ruler on top of your head at the point where it meets the wall. Mark the wall lightly with a pencil at this point and measure down to the floor.

7 Finished length (skirt)

Put on your shoes and measure from your waist down to the required hem length.

8 Finished length (pants)

Put on your shoes and measure from the waist to the floor at the side of the body.

9 Sleeve length

Put your hand on your hip and measure from your shoulder to your wrist bone.

10 Shoulder length

Measure from the nape of your neck down to your shoulder edge.

11 Crotch length

Measure from your waist at your back through your legs (11a) to your belly button at the front (11b).

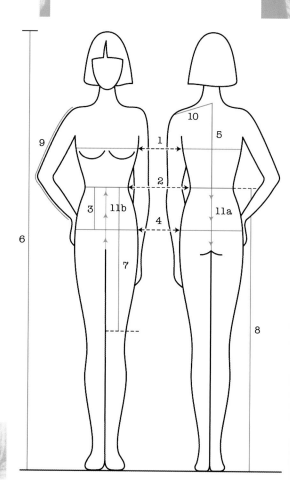

How to make a mannequin bodice

Dress forms can be very expensive, so here is a homemade alternative—a taped bodice that molds to your body, which you can then use to create clothes that are a perfect fit!

Making a mannequin bodice, step 2

YOU WILL NEED
- Two old T-shirts
- Gaffer or masking tape, 2 in. (5 cm) wide
- Permanent marker pen
- Strong scissors (not too pointed on the ends would be helpful as you don't want to hurt or be hurt!)
- 20 in. (50 cm) string and a plum line (string with a weight on the end of it!)

1 Put both T-shirts on over your regular bra: the bottom one is for your modesty and the top one will act as a base for the bodice and will be cut off later. If you do not have a spare T-shirt, you could use a plastic bin liner in place of the top T-shirt.

2 Ask a friend to wrap the tape snugly around your figure, starting just above the curve of your hip and then working upward. You may need to fold the tape slightly just above the waistline to accommodate the curve of the waistline. If you find it easier, cut long strips of gaffer tape to cover the front and then the back of your bodice. The tape should not be too tight, just snug. It shouldn't squash you uncomfortably in any way.

3 When you reach your armpits, tear or cut the tape and run pieces over the shoulders from as close to the neck as you can manage to up to 7 in. (18 cm) along your shoulder seam measured from the nape of your neck.

4 Now apply tape over the front and back of the bodice, running it down from the shoulder to about 6 in. (15 cm) below your waist.

5 Using a permanent marker pen, draw a high neckline on the tape, front and back.

6 Hold the plum line down your center front and get your friend to draw carefully down the center front line. Wrap the string around your waistline and get your friend draw around this line, too. Using the plum line again, draw down the center back line. You will be using these drawn lines as a guide in the future.

7 Get your friend to carefully cut the taped T-shirt off you, cutting up from the bottom of the center back line. Cut along the drawn neckline, too.

8 Make sure that the bottom of the bodice is even so that it will sit comfortably on your work surface. Put a pillow in the center of the bodice and tape the cut center back line up again. Now you are ready to pin fabric onto your improvised dress form!

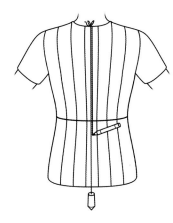

Making a mannequin bodice, step 4

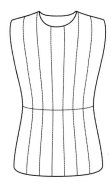

Making a mannequin bodice, step 6

Making a mannequin bodice, step 8

Understanding patterns

Commercial patterns use standard markings to indicate how to align different pieces and to show where extras such as zippers and buttons need to go. Once you understand what these pattern markings mean, you will have a better grasp of how garments are put together and will understand the importance of using markings when you make your own patterns.

Work from the wrong side of the fabric unless otherwise indicated. Patterns often contain pieces for several garments, so the pieces are usually numbered so that you can tell quickly which ones you need. In the general directions (which are normally given on a separate piece of paper), follow the cutting layouts: tinted pieces mean that the fabric is right side down and the white mean that the fabric right side up.

Cutting-out markings

These markings help you to cut out and alter the pattern pieces and lay out the pattern pieces on the fabric in the correct way.

Cutting lines
Multi-sized patterns have different cutting lines for each size; make sure you follow the correct one by checking how your measurements match up with the measurements on the back of the pattern envelope.

Alteration lines
If you want to lengthen or shorten a pattern piece, the double parallel lines on the pattern will indicate the point at which you need to do this.

Straight grain or grainline
A straight line with an arrowhead at each end means place the pattern piece on the straight grain or the bias grainline of the fabric (see page 113).

Fold
This marking indicates that you should place the pattern piece exactly on the folded edge of the fabric.

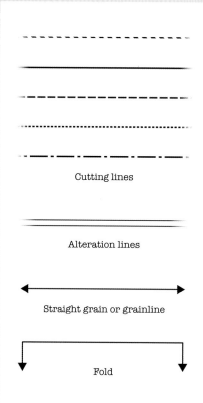

Cutting lines

Alteration lines

Straight grain or grainline

Fold

Construction markings

These are used to help you match pieces of fabric together and to show where zippers, buttons, and pockets are to be positioned.

Balance notches
Balance notches are used to help you match pieces of fabric together—for example, to match the center front of a waistband to the center front of a skirt. They are normally drawn as diamonds or triangles.

Dots
Dots are used to show the position of pockets, buttons, zippers, and eyelets. They are normally drawn as circles.

Darts
Darts are always the first pattern detail that you should attend to. The markings (which may be notches or dots) should be matched up; solid or broken lines are stitching lines that meet at a point. I use tailor's tacks (see page 113) to mark darts, as they are easy to match up; alternatively, you could use tailor's chalk or a tracing wheel and carbon paper.

Balance notches

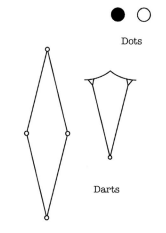

Dots

Darts

Transferring marks from pattern to fabric

Before you remove the paper pattern from the fabric, you need to transfer the pattern markings to the fabric. One way to do this is to place dressmaker's carbon paper between the paper pattern and the fabric and to go over the marks with a pencil or a tracing wheel. Other methods are shown below.

Marking notches
Notches can be marked by cutting around the outer edges of the diamonds or by making a small snip about ⅛ in. (2–3 mm) deep into the seam allowances at the triangles. You can also buy a notcher, which will cut a square notch into the seam allowance which is useful for marking balance marks.

Marking dots, circles, and darts
Make a small hole in the pattern at the dot position and mark the dot with a chalk pencil. If you have a double layer of fabric, at the dot position push a pin straight down through the fabric layers and mark the dot on the bottom layer of fabric.

Marking notches

Marking dots, circles, and darts

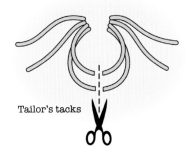

Tailor's tacks

Tailor's tacks
Tailor's tacks are usually used for transferring markings when two layers of fabric are involved. Using a double thread, bring the needle through both layers, leaving a long tail, then work a small back stitch and bring the needle through, leaving a loop. Cut the threads, leaving long ends. Cut the loop of the back stitch and remove the pattern. Carefully pull the two layers of fabric apart and snip the threads between them, leaving tufts of thread as a marker point. A continuous line of tailor's tacks can be used to mark features such as a center front line or a fold on a pleat. Simplified tailor's tacks (uneven tacking) can be useful for marking single layers of fabric and for marking fold, center, and pleat lines.

Fabric grain

First, you need to understand a few basic fabric terms.

Selvage: This is the border that runs lengthwise down both sides of a piece of fabric. It is usually cut off, since (as it is woven more tightly than the rest to prevent the edges from fraying) it might pucker when the fabric is cleaned.

Grain (straight and crosswise): The "grain" describes the direction in which the threads run in a woven fabric. The straight grain runs parallel to the selvage. The crosswise grain runs from one selvage to the other. The bias grain lies at a 45-degree angle to both the straight and crosswise grains. The straight and crosswise grains of a woven fabric are very firm, so the fabric has very little give in these directions. Fabric cut on the bias has the most give.

When you copy or draw up a pattern piece and pin it to the fabric, make sure that you get the grainline correct, as this has a huge effect on how the fabric will hang when the garment is made up.

Cutting out

Following the few simple guidelines below will ensure success in your cutting!

1 Make sure that the grain lines on pattern pieces run parallel to the selvage by measuring from each end of the grain-line arrow to the selvedge and adjusting the position of the pattern pieces until the distances are equal.

2 Check that any fold lines on the paper pattern pieces are placed exactly on the fold of the fabric.

3 Pin your paper pattern pieces to the fabric, spacing the pins about 8 in. (20 cm) apart.

4 Carefully cut around the edges of the pattern pieces, taking care to cut around any balance marks (see page 112).

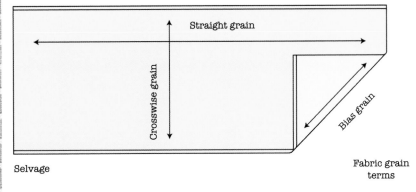

Selvage

Straight grain

Crosswise grain

Bias grain

Selvage

Fabric grain terms

Unpicking seams

Whether you are unpicking a dress that you want to magically transform into something else or are unpicking a seam that you had got wrong first time around (it happens to us all, so don't beat yourself up about it!), here are a few useful guidelines.

- Most unpicking can be done with a pair of small, sharp-pointed scissors. Alternatively, you can use a seam ripper.
- Pull the seam gently apart to expose the stitches before cutting into the threads. If the seam is sewn on a fragile or light fabric, snip into one thread and pull the threads out gently. If the item was sewn using small stitches, then it may help to lift one stitch up with a pin to access the thread.
- Occasionally you may not be able to access the stitched seam from the wrong side. If this is the case, work from the least visible part of the item—for example, if you are unpicking a side seam, start from the bottom of the seam.
- Try to avoid pulling the seams apart. More often than not, the fabric will tear and could make your potentially perfect dress into something that cannot be repaired.

Trimming and neatening seam allowances

Trimming and neatening seam allowances reduces bulk and provides a professional-looking finish.

Trimming seam allowances

Excess fabric in seam allowances can cause ridges and a lumpy finish. Once you've stitched your seam, trim the seam allowances using one of the methods shown below.

Right-angled corner
Cut diagonally across the corner of the seam turnings, taking care not to cut through the stitches. Turn the piece right side out, then use the tip of small pointed scissors or a knitting needle to push out the point to a sharp corner.

Acute corner
Cut across the corner close to the stitching, as for a right-angled corner, then trim away another slither of fabric from each side so that, when the corner is turned right side out, the seam allowances will lie flat.

Layering seams
Trim the seam allowances to graduating widths so that the narrowest seam allowance is ³⁄₁₆ in. (5 mm) wide and the widest lies next to the most visible seam edge.

Notching and snipping curved seams
On inward (concave) curves, cut small wedges of fabric out of the seam allowance to allow the curve to lie flat. On outward or convex curves (not shown), simply cut straight snips into the seam allowances.

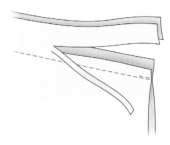

Layering seams

Right-angled corner

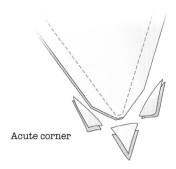

Acute corner

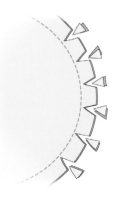

Notching and snipping curved seams

Neatening seam allowances

Neatening the edges of seam allowances prevents them from fraying and helps them lay flat. Don't be tempted to miss out this stage, as it gives a neat, professional finish.

The seams on commercially sewn clothes are often finished with overlock stitching. If you're serious about making your own clothes, you can buy a special sewing machine called a serger or overlocker, which can stitch the seam, oversew the edge, and trim off any excess fabric all at the same time—but for most people, one of the methods shown below will be perfectly adequate.

Plain zigzag using an overcasting foot
Trim the edges to remove any fraying, then consult your instruction manual for the correct stitch settings. Place the edge of the fabric under the overcasting foot, with the pin on the foot along the edge of the fabric, and stitch along the raw edge.

Zigzag without an overcasting foot
Set your machine to a medium width and short length zigzag, then stitch 1⁄8 in. (3 mm) from the edge of the seam allowance. Trim off the outer edge of the fabric, close to the stitching.

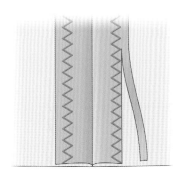

Plain zigzag using an overcasting foot

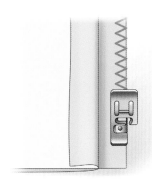

Zigzag without an overcasting foot

Binding seam allowances

On stretch fabrics, the seam allowances are often bound (see page 119) to help reinforce the seam. This method was used for the Hot Pants on page 80; it is also suitable for seaming heavy fabrics.

Sewing tip

If your machine does not do zigzag stitch, straight stitch along the edges about 1⁄4 in. (6 mm) from the edge, then trim the edges with pinking shears.

Darts

A dart is simply a fold in a piece of fabric that is stitched to help give a garment shape.

Darts are stitched to a point and may be either curved or straight, as they are designed to fit the contours of the body. When sewing an outfit, the darts are normally stitched first.

Darts are most commonly placed at the waistline, shoulder, and bust. The best way to follow them and get them accurate is to use a tracing wheel or tailor's tacks (if more than one layer of fabric) on either side of the dart to ensure that they are stitched correctly.

Plain darts

A plain dart is shown on patterns as a triangle with two stitchlines and sometimes a central fold line; there may also be two notches at the edge and a dot at the point (see page 112).

1 Transfer the dart markings to the wrong side of your fabric (see page 113). Working from the wrong side, fold the dart in half through the center, matching the stitchlines and other markings. Pin and baste (tack) the dart in place.

2 Starting from the wide end of the dart, stitch toward the point, reverse stitching at the start to secure. To finish, take the last couple of stitches a thread's width from the fold. Cut the thread ends, leaving at least 4 in. (10 cm). Knot the thread ends, but do not pull too tightly. Trim the thread ends to ⅜ in. (1 cm).

3 Lay the dart flat on an ironing board, with the fold of the dart to one side, and iron toward the point.

4 Open out the fabric and press the dart in the direction instructed. This is usually toward the center for waist darts and toward the waist on bust darts.

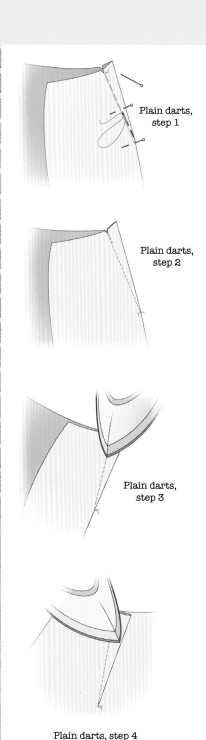

Plain darts, step 1

Plain darts, step 2

Plain darts, step 3

Plain darts, step 4

Contour darts

These long darts, which have a point at each end, are used on fitted and semi-fitted dresses. The widest part fits into the waistline and then tapers off to fit the bust and the hip, or the back and the hip. They are usually shown on patterns as a long, thin diamond, with stitchlines and a series of dots to be matched.

1 Transfer the dart markings to the wrong side of your fabric (see page 113). With the right sides of the fabric together, fold along the center of the dart. Match and pin the dots and stitchlines at the waist first, then at the points, and then at any marks in between. Baste (tack) the dart in place just inside the stitching lines and remove the pins.

2 Stitch the dart in two halves, starting at the middle (waistline) and stitching toward the point. Instead of reverse stitching to start, overlap the stitching at the waist and tie the thread ends at both points.

3 Remove the basting (tacking) stitches and clip into the dart at the waistline to within ⅛ in. (3 mm) of the stitchline; this will allow for the dart to curve smoothly at the waist. Press the dart flat as it was stitched, then press it toward the center of the garment.

Contour darts, step 1

Contour darts, step 2

Contour darts, step 3

Gathering

Gathers are tiny, soft folds that are formed by drawing up fabric into a smaller area. The fabric is normally gathered to one half or one third of the original width. Gathers were used in many of the projects—for example the Patchwork Ranch Skirt (page 92) and the Folklore Dress (page 86).

Machine gathering is worked by stitching two rows of long machine stitches across the edge to be gathered; the fabric is then gathered up by pulling on the bobbin threads. The parallel rows of stitching should be stitched across the grain.

1 Set your machine to a longer stitch—¹⁄₁₆ in. (2 mm) for lightweight fabrics to ⅛ in. (3 mm) for heavier fabrics. Loosen the upper tension slightly (refer to your instruction manual). Leaving long thread ends, work two parallel rows of gathering stitches ¼ in (6 mm) apart within the seam allowance along the fabric edge, with the outer row of stitching a thread's width from the seam line and stitching between any seams where necessary.

2 Divide the stitched area and the edge to which it will be attached into four or more equal sections and mark them with a pin. With right sides together, pin the stitched edge to the corresponding edge, matching marker pins.

3 At one end, secure the bobbin threads by twisting them around a pin in a figure eight. At the other edge, pull both gathering threads together and gently ease the gathers along the threads. When the gathered edge fits the pieces to which it is going to be stitched, secure the thread ends around another pin, as before. On long edges, gather the fabric from each end toward the center, rather than trying to gather across the entire piece in one go.

4 Unwind the thread ends around each end pin and knot each set together to secure them; trim the ends to about 1 in. (2.5 cm). With the gathered side up, baste (tack) the two layers together between the two rows of stitching, using short stitches. Remove the pins.

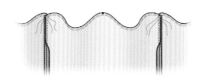

Gathering, step 1

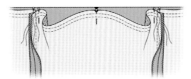

Gathering, step 2

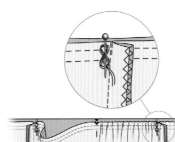

Gathering, step 3

Gathering, step 4

5 Return your machine stitch length and tension to the appropriate setting. With the gathered side on top, reverse stitching to start and finish, machine stitch the gathered edge to the corresponding edge, holding the fabric on either side of the machine foot as you sew to prevent the gathers from being pushed and stitched into pleats. Remove the basting (tacking) stitches.

6 Diagonally trim matched seam allowances to reduce bulk (see page 114). Using the tip of the iron, press the seam allowances flat as they were stitched—but do not press the gathers. Neaten the seam allowances together. Open the sections out and press the seam toward the flat section. Press the gathers by sliding the point of the iron into the gathers toward the seam.

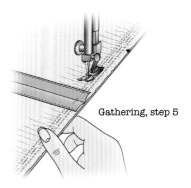

Gathering, step 5

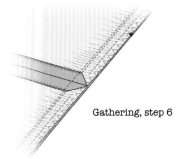

Gathering, step 6

Ruching

Ruching works on the same principle as gathering, although it is not necessarily done on a seam line. The aim is to create fullness and add drama to a piece of clothing: see the Prairie Dress (page 76). It can be done on small areas, such as waistline or bustline.

Facings

A facing is used to finish the raw edges around an opening of a garment—the neckline, armholes, and center front of a shirt or blouse.

When the garment edge is straight (for example, the center front of a blouse), the facing may be cut as part of the main garment piece and then simply folded to the wrong side; this is known as an integrated facing. On a curved edge, such as a neckline or armhole, a separate shaped facing is required (see below).

Making your own pattern for a shaped neckline facing

1 Turn the garment wrong side out, with the front facing up.

2 Place tracing or brown parcel paper over the neckline of the garment and pin it on.

3 Trace the neckline exactly onto the paper.

4 Most facings are 2–2½ in. (5–6 cm) deep. Measure this distance down from the neckline that you have drawn and draw another line that exactly follows the curve of the neckline.

5 Mark balance notches (see page 112) on both the paper and the garment.

6 Remove the paper from the garment. Measure and mark a line ⅝ in. (1.5 cm) above the drawn neckline; this is the neckline seam allowance.

7 Repeat steps 1–6 at the back of the garment.

8 Lay the paper tracings flat and cut out the patterns, making sure that your curves are smooth.

9 Pin the patterns to the facing fabric and cut out; the grain direction depends on the curve of the neckline/armhole opening. If you don't have matching fabric, aim for a fabric of the same or a slightly lighter weight, so that the facing doesn't create too much bulk.

10 Machine zigzag stitch along the outer edge of the facing to prevent it from fraying.

11 If you want to apply interfacing to the facings to maintain the shape, apply it to each piece separately, stay stitching ⅛ in. (3 mm) inside the seamline of each facing.

12 Join the front and back neck facings across the shoulder seams, trim and notch the seam allowances (see page 114), and press open the seams.

13 With right sides together, pin, baste (tack), and machine stitch the facing to the garment along the neck seamline.

14 Trim and notch the seam allowances all the way around the neckline.

15 Place the seam wrong side up on a sleeve board or the curved edge of your ironing board and press the neckline seam open. Then press all the seam allowances toward the facing.

Making a pattern for a shaped neckline facing, step 13

Making a pattern for a shaped neckline facing, step 14

Making a pattern for a shaped neckline facing, step 15

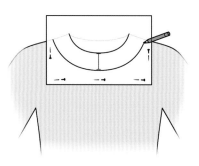

Making a pattern for a shaped neckline facing, step 4

Bias binding

Bias binding is a strip of bias-cut fabric with folded edges for binding curved or straight edges. It can be used for both clothing and for home furnishings.

Ready-made bias binding is normally available in just two widths: ½–⅝ in. (12–15 mm) and ¾–1 in. (20–25 mm). It is more satisfying to make your own binding, as you can use fabric that will match your project exactly.

To make things easier, you can buy a metal gadget for making bias binding from a notions (haberdashery) store. Just feed the binding material through a curved channel and hey presto! It magically reappears as bias binding on the other end.

Making bias binding

Bias binding is made from strips of fabric cut diagonally across the fabric's width, following the bias grain (see page 113).

1 First, find the bias direction. Fold the raw edge of the fabric over to form a triangle that lies parallel to one of the selvedges. Press and cut along this line: this is the bias line which you must work from.

2 Draw chalk lines parallel to the bias to your required width: this should be four times the finished flat width of the binding. Cut along these lines until you have enough strips to go all around the edges of your project.

3 To join two bias strips together, cut the ends that are to be joined at a 45 degree angle. Place one strip on top of the other, right sides together, and stitch the pieces together diagonally—that is, on the straight grain. Trim the seam turnings and press the seam open.

4 With wrong sides facing, press the strip in half along its length. Open the strip out flat and press the long raw edges over to the wrong side to meet at the central pressline.

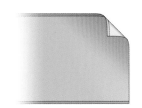

Making bias binding, step 1

Making bias binding, step 2

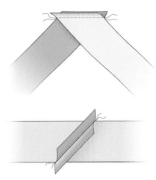

Making bias binding, step 3

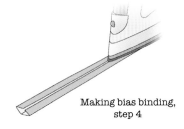

Making bias binding, step 4

Applying binding by machine, step 1

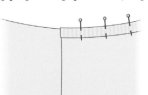

Applying binding by machine, step 2

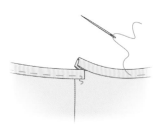

Applying binding by machine, step 3

Applying binding

There are two methods of applying binding: machining and slip hemming. The machine method is used when both sides of the item will be seen. The slip-hemming method can be used when one side of the binding will not be visible—around the neckline of a garment, for example.

Machine method

1 Cut a strip of binding four times the required finished width. Turn back the starting end of the binding by ⅜ in. (1 cm) and press. Fold the strip in half lengthwise, making one side slightly wider than the other. Press. Open out. Fold the raw long edges in to meet the central press line and press again.

2 Align the short pressed end with a garment seam, if there is one, then sandwich the fabric edge between the binding layers, with the wider part of the binding underneath. Pin the binding in place.

3 Trim off the excess binding, allowing for ⅜ in. (1 cm) to underlap the folded starting end. Baste (tack) the binding into place. Working from the right side, machine stitch the binding in place stitching close to the binding edge. Remove the basting (tacking) stitches and press.

Slip hem method

1 Open out one fold on the binding and pin to the garment edge, with right sides together and aligning the raw edges. Turn back the starting edge by ⅜ in. (1 cm) and align it with a seam, if there is one. Pin and baste (tack) the binding in place, reverse stitching at the start and finishing the stitching about 2 in. (5 cm) from the starting point.

2 Trim away the excess binding, leaving ⅜ in. (1 cm) to underlap the folded starting end. Machine stitch the end in place along the top foldline through all layers. Press the seam allowances toward the binding. Bring the opposite folded edge of the binding over to meet the seamline, enclosing the raw edge. Pin in place. Slip hem (see page 109) the folded edge to the seamline.

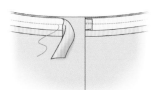

Applying binding by slip hemming, step 1

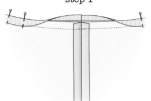

Applying binding by slip hemming, step 2

Waistbands

Knowing how to make a waistband is a really useful technique—and it doesn't have to be scary! I've used two different types of waistband in this book: a straight waistband and a waistband with a shaped facing.

Straight waistband

A straight waistband is the most popular type. It is designed to sit on your waist snugly with a little ease. Straight waistbands are cut on the straight grain of the fabric and are rectangular in shape. The finished depth should not exceed 2 in. (5 cm).

If you are cutting your own waistband without a pattern, cut a piece of fabric the circumference of your waist plus about 3 in. (7.5 cm) for an overlap and twice the required depth of the finished waistband. Remember to include balance marks (see page 112) on both the waistband and the waistband edge of the garment.

1 Cut a piece of interfacing half the width of the waistband. Following the manufacturer's instructions, apply the interfacing to the wrong side of the waistband. Press the waistband in half lengthwise, with wrong sides together. Open the waistband out flat again and then, with right sides together, pin, baste (tack), and machine stitch the waistband to the waist edge of the garment, matching the balance marks.

2 Fold the waistband in half along the pressline, with right sides together. Pin, baste (tack), and machine stitch across the short end of the waistband at the left-hand zipper opening, from the folded edge to the waistband stitchline. At the other end, pin, baste, and machine stitch around the waistband extension from the folded edge to meet the waistband stitchline.

3 Snip the corners of the waistband seam turnings to reduce bulk (see page 114), then turn the waistband right side out. Press the loose waistband edge to the wrong side and slip hem (see page 109) the pressed edge along the machine stitches, enclosing the raw edges. Attach fastenings to close the waist (see page 124).

Straight waistband, step 1

Straight waistband, step 2

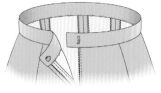

Straight waistband, step 3

Waistband with a shaped facing

Waist facings provide a smooth finish that does not extend above the waistline edge.

1 Following the manufacturer's instructions, apply iron-on interfacing to the waist facing. Stitch the side seams together and press open. Neaten the lower edge (see page 115).

2 With right sides together, pin the facing to the garment, matching all balance marks. Pin cotton tape over the waist seamline and baste (tack) through all layers. Stitch the seam, then layer the seam allowances (see page 114).

Waistband with a shaped facing, step 1

Waistband with a shaped facing, step 2

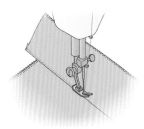

Waistband with a shaped facing, step 3

Waistband with a shaped facing, step 4

3 Press the facing and the seam allowances away from the garment. Working from the right side, stitch the seam allowances to the facing.

4 Turn the facing to the inside and press along the waist edge. Hand stitch the lower edge of the facing to the garment side seams and darts. Turn the seam allowances under at the facing ends and pin in place. Slip hem the facing ends to the zipper tape, then attach fasteners to close the waist.

Casings

Casings are a fabric tunnel made to enclose elastic or a drawstring. They are useful on waistbands, as they can be adjusted to fit your changing waistline or to give a different look, but they can also be used on cuffs and pant hems.

There are two main types of casing: fold-down casings, in which the fabric is folded under into a hem and applied casings, for which a separate strip of fabric is required. A casing needs to be ¼ in. (6 mm) wider than whatever is being threaded through it.

Flat fold-down casing

In this type of casing, the ends are left open so that a drawstring can be threaded through. A flat fold-down casing was used on the Out of Africa Jumpsuit and the sleeves of the Sweetheart Top (pages 28 and 64).

1 Fold and press the hem allowance to the wrong side, the trim away any excess hem allowance to measure ¼ in. (6 mm). Fold over the casing depth to the wrong side, then pin and baste (tack) in place.

2 Machine stitch the lower edge of the casing in place, reverse stitching at each end of secure. Work a second row of stitching along the folded edge, again reverse stitching to secure.

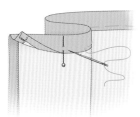

Flat fold-down casing, step 1

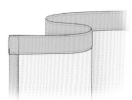

Flat fold-down casing, step 2

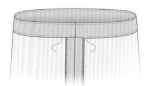

Circular fold-down casing

Circular fold-down casing

On a circular casing, you need to leave a gap so that you can insert elastic or a drawstring.

1 Follow step 1 of the Flat fold-down casing, then machine stitch around the lower edge, leaving a gap. Work a second row of stitching close to the folded edge, overlapping the ends of the stitching to secure. Insert the elastic or drawstring (see page 122), then machine stitch or slipstitch the gap closed.

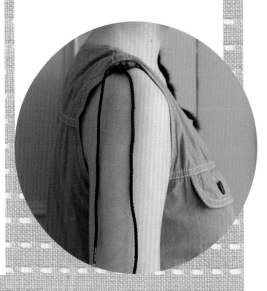

Applied casing

These casings are normally applied in a circle; you do not need to leave a gap for inserting elastic, as the ends of the strip will meet at a seam, leaving you with an opening.

1 Cut a strip of fabric on the straight grain if your casing is straight, or on the bias grain if it needs to curve. Neaten the lower long edge and trim the top seam allowance to ⅜ in. (1 cm). With right sides facing, pin, baste (tack), and machine stitch the casing to the garment, overlapping the stitching ends to secure. Trim the seam allowance to ¼ in. (6 mm) and press the seam open.

2 Fold over and press the casing to the wrong side of the garment. Pin, baste (tack), and machine stitch the lower edge in place. Work a second row of topstitching just below the top edge of the casing, overlapping the ends to secure.

Threading a casing

This technique can be used with elastic, drawstring, or cord.

On both fold-down and applied casings
1 Attach a safety pin to one end of the elastic, drawstring, or cord, and pin the other end to the garment (unless you are using a delicate fabric such as silk, as the safety pin would leave a hole; in this case, simply make sure that the other end of the elastic does not disappear into the channel). Thread the safety pin through the casing, making sure the elastic or drawstring does not twist as you do so. Overlap the ends by ⅜ in. (1 cm) and work several rows of zigzag stitch to join the ends together.

On a fold-down casing
2 If using elastic, stretch it slightly to keep your work flat, then machine stitch or slipstitch across the gap, overlapping the stitching at each end and taking care not to catch the elastic or drawstring material as you sew.

On an applied casing
2 Slipstitch the opening edges together, taking care not to catch the elastic or drawstring material as you sew.

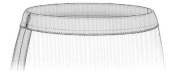

Applied casing, step 1

Applied casing, step 2

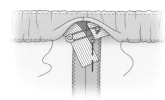

Threading a casing, step 1 (on both fold-down and applied casings)

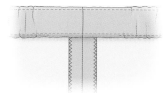

Threading a casing, step 2 (on a fold-down casing)

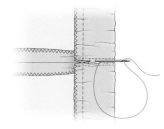

Threading a casing, step 2 (on an applied casing)

Set-in sleeves

Although there are many types of sleeve, set-in sleeves are the most widely used; most are made from a single piece of fabric. Follow these step-by-step instructions and you will have mastered one of the more fiddly aspects of sewing.

1 To create the gathering (easing in) of the sleeve head you need to work two parallel rows of stitching around the top of each sleeve head, between the outer dots. Set your machine to the longest stitch length and stitch two parallel lines—the first a thread's width from the seamline and the second ⅛ in. (3 mm) from the first stitching line. With right sides together, pin, baste (tack), and machine stitch (using a medium/regular stitch length) the sleeve underarm seam. Press the seam open and neaten the seam allowances separately. Turn the sleeve right side out.

Set-in sleeves, step 1

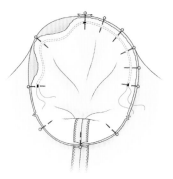

Set-in sleeves, step 2

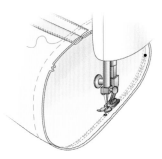

Set-in sleeves, step 3

2 With right sides together, aligning the top dot with the shoulder seam and the underarm seam with the side seam of the garment, pin the sleeve to the armhole. Gently pull up the stitching around the top of the sleeve head so that the sleeve fits the armhole and pin it in place at ⅜-in. (1-cm) intervals. Baste (tack) the sleeve in place. Press over a tailor's ham to remove any puckering.

3 With right sides together, starting at the underarm seam, stitch the sleeve to the armhole along the seamline. Remove the basting (tacking) stitches and neaten the seam allowances.

Collars

Collars, like sleeves, come in all sorts of shapes and sizes, the simplest and most common of which is the flat collar. Flat collars may be made up of one unit that fits the neckline (usually on a front-opening garment such as a blouse) or two units if the collar is split at the front and back (common if the garment has a back opening—for example, a dress). Both types consist of two layers of fabric (an under collar and a top collar) and are attached in the same way.

1 Staystitch (see page 110) the neck edge of the garment and stitch, press, and neaten any seams and darts that intersect the neckline before you attach the collar.

2 Apply interfacing to the wrong side of the top collar. With right sides together, pin, baste (tack), and machine stitch the top collar to the under collar, leaving the neck edge open. Trim and notch the curved seam allowance (see page 114).

3 Turn the collar right side out. Press the collar, rolling the seam slightly to the underside. Pin and baste (tack) the collar neck edges together.

4 With right sides uppermost, matching the ends of the collar to the center front (and/or center back) at the neckline seam, pin and baste (tack) the collar to the neckline of the garment.

5 Apply interfacing to the wrong side of the appropriate facing pieces. With right sides together, pin, baste (tack), and machine stitch the front facings to the back facing at the shoulder seams. Press the seams open, then neaten the outer edge of the joined facings.

6 Pin and baste (tack) the joined facings to the collar and the garment at the neck and front edges, matching the pattern markings, shoulder seams, and front hem edges; the collar will now be sandwiched between the facings and the garment. Stitch the pieces together. Trim and notch the seam allowances (see page 114). Turn the facing to the right side and tease out the front corners.

7 With the facing right side up, stitch the seam allowances to the facing close to the neck seamline. Press the facing to the inside of the garment. Slip hem the neatened outer edge of the facing to the shoulder seams.

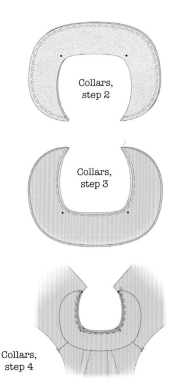

Collars, step 2

Collars, step 3

Collars, step 4

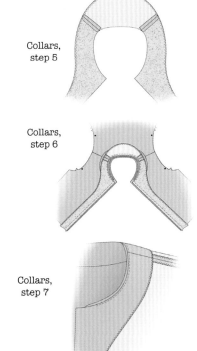

Collars, step 5

Collars, step 6

Collars, step 7

Fastenings

Fastenings appear in most of these projects. They can be just quietly doing their job behind the scenes (or the garment!), but most of them are out working and looking good, too! Why not take out a broken, concealed zipper and replace it with a colored, exposed one to give a regular garment a modern and edgy twist—or, if you feel that your old summer dress has had too many outings, change the buttons and add zippers to the shoulder seams?

Buttons

Where do I start? I can love a button so much that I can design an entire outfit around it! Buttons can be attached in many ways and their fastenings can be varied, too.

For a button fastening, you can sew a buttonhole (if you feel able to do this), sew a button on top of a snap fastening, or make button loops (see the Pretty in Pink dress, page 68) for a pretty touch.

Alternatively, you can sew a button on just for decoration (see the Circus Skirt on page 52 or the Sleeveless Thermal Top on page 10).

You can give the same button different looks by the way in which you sew it on, too: matching or contrasting thread, machine or buttonhole thread, with straight or cross stitches. The choice is yours!

Zippers

There are three main types of zipper: conventional, concealed, and open-ended.

Conventional zippers
These have either metal or plastic teeth, and are available in a variety of lengths, normally at 2-in. (5-cm) increments. They are enclosed in the garment at a seam and can be shortened. The zipper is permanently closed at the base with a "stopper" and locks at the top for a firm fastening. This type was used in the Silk Doily Top at the shoulder seam (page 24).

Open-ended zippers
These zippers open up at both ends and tend to be used on the center front of a jacket or coat. These are the only zips which cannot be shortened with this function. An open-ended zipper is inserted in much the same way as a conventional zipper (see below), but it can also be sewn with the zipper teeth exposed. Make sure that the two seams are perfectly aligned before you stitch them. This zipper was used in the 1970s Cape (page 104).

Concealed zippers
These have no teeth showing on the right side and are inserted with a special zipper foot attached to your machine. The zipper is inserted before the seam is stitched. It is stitched in place from the wrong side and it is harder to sew in place well. It is a good idea to master conventional zippers before attempting a concealed one. I used this type in the Sunshine Dress (page 100).

Conventional zippers

Open-ended zippers

Concealed zippers

Inserting a centered zipper

Centered zippers are used on centered openings, such as the back of a dress. The zipper is placed between the two edges of the opening, with the stitching spaced evenly down both sides. This method can be used for both conventional and open-ended zippers.

1 Stitch the garment seam up to the zipper notch, reverse stitching to secure. Adjust your machine stitch to the largest size and machine baste (tack) the zipper opening edges together, without reverse stitching at the ends. Snip the basting stitches at ½-in. (12-mm) intervals along the zipper opening. Neaten the seam turnings (see page 115) and press the seam open.

2 Place the zipper face down on the seam turnings, so that the zipper teeth run centrally down the seam and the bottom "stopper" is just below the notch. Pin and baste (tack) the zipper in place.

3 Working from the right side of the garment, with a regular stitch length on your machine, stitch the zipper in place. Have the zipper foot to the left of the needle; starting just below the zipper at the seam line, work three or four stitches across the bottom, pivot your work, and stitch up to the top of the zipper. Reverse stitch at each end to secure.

4 Re-position the zipper foot to the right of the needle; starting again at the base of the zipper, stitch the other side in place, as before. Remove the basting (tacking) stitches and unpick the seam covering the zipper teeth.

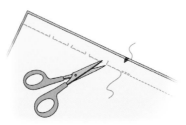
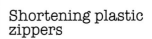

Inserting a centered zipper, step 1

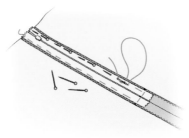

Inserting a centered zipper, step 2

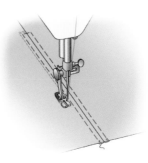

Inserting a centered zipper, step 3

Inserting a centered zipper, step 4

Shortening plastic zippers

Measure the length of the opening to be fitted with the zipper and mark this length on the zipper tape. Make a new bottom stop at this point by stitching the bar of a hook-and-bar fastening, machine zigzag stitching with the stitch length set to zero, or whipstitching 8 or 9 times securely across the new end point by hand. Cut off the excess zipper teeth and tape about ⅝ in. (1.5 cm) below the new stop.

It is possible to shorten metal zippers, too—but this requires the use of fairly heavy-duty pliers to cut through the teeth and re-crimp the end stop onto the tape.

Dyeing fabric

Fabric can be dyed to mask stains, give an item of clothing new life, or simply to keep up with current color trends. Why not go through your wardrobe and pick out some worn-out or unworn pieces and throw them into the dye bath?

If you want the color to turn out exactly the same as the one shown on the box of dye, make sure that the fabric is as close to 100 percent natural fiber as possible (cotton, wool, or silk), as natural fibers will absorb the dye well. A fabric with a lower cotton content can be dyed, but the results will be lighter in shade.

Another thing to bear in mind is the stitching. Your denim jacket may be 100 percent cotton—but if the stitching has been done in polyester thread, it will not absorb the dye and will remain the original color (although this can sometimes add to the look). If you are concerned about what the end result will be, then do a patch test first by cutting a piece of the fabric out of the hem and dyeing it in a cup (one that you are not going to drink out of again!).

Rubber gloves, an apron, salt, and a mask are essential. If you're seriously interested in dyeing, it's also worth looking at a color wheel to find out how colors work, as there is a real science to dyeing and color mixing.

Before you start, make sure that you have the right amount of dye to match the weight of your fabric and enough salt to fix it into place. The instructions on the box of dye will tell you how much you need. You can buy machine dyes and hot-water and cold-water dyes.

1 Remove any visible marks or stains from the fabric, which could prevent it from absorbing the color evenly, then wash and dry the fabric as normal. Do not use fabric softeners, as this will create a sheen.

2 Dampen the garment and make sure that it is wet all over, so that it can absorb the color evenly.

3 For hot- and cold-water dyes, weigh the dye, then mix it with hot water in a small container, stirring well so that all of the powder mixes in—otherwise you will end up with dark marks on your fabric. Weigh the correct amount of salt and mix this with hot water, again stirring well. For machine dyes, simply weigh out the correct amount of dye and salt and put them straight into the drum of your washing machine with your pre-dampened fabric to be dyed.

4 Unfold the damp fabric, place it in the dye bath or washing machine, and dye it for the recommended time, or longer if you wish—but bear in mind that there is a limit to how dark the fabric will go.

5 Take the fabric out and rinse it extremely well in plenty of warm or cold water.

6 Wash the fabric with a light detergent to get rid of any remaining dye; the colors may run, so wash the fabric on its own. If you've dyed the fabric in your washing machine, it's a good idea to put the machine through at least one wash cycle with nothing in the drum, to make sure that you've got rid of all the dye before you do your next load of delicate whites!

7 Hang the fabric outside on a washing line or above the bath tub and allow it to dry naturally.

8 When you've transformed your newly dyed garment or fabric into a new piece of clothing, always wash it separately in case the color runs.

SUPPLIERS

My advice to you is that when you find a reliable supplier, stick with them and support them!

UK

BOROVICK FABRICS
16 Berwick Street
London W1F OHP
Tel: 020 7437 2180
www.borovickfabricsltd.co.uk
Stocked to the ceiling with
fabrics to die for!

CALICO LAINE
Tel: 0151 336 5982
www.calicolaine.co.uk
This Cheshire-based online
supplier of sewing materials
has a good range and reliably
fast delivery times. They also
have a telephone sales line
manned by very friendly and
helpful people.

THE CLOTH HOUSE
47 Berwick Street
London W1F 8SJ
Tel: 020 7437 5155
www.clothhouse.com
Stocks an extensive
collection of fabrics, from
woollens, linens, and cottons
to fine jerseys and silks. Also
supplies by mail order.

THE COTTON PATCH
1283–1285 Stratford Road
Hall Green
Birmingham B28 9AJ
Tel: 0121 702 2840
www.cottonpatch.co.uk
Shop and online store
specializing in patchwork and
quilting fabrics, batting
(wadding), and notions
(haberdashery). If you're
looking for print fabrics on a
particular theme, this is a
great place to start.

DUTTONS FOR BUTTONS
Oxford Street
Harrogate
North Yorkshire HG1 1QE
01423 502 092
www.duttonsforbuttons.co.uk
All the buttons, zippers,
trimmings, and notions you
are ever likely to need! There
are two other shops, in Ilkley
and York, as well as a reliable
mail-order service.

FABRICS PLUS
19 Badminton Road
Downend
Bristol BS16 6BB
Tel: 0117 329 3857
www.fabrics-plus.co.uk
Notions (haberdashery) and
fabric supplier.

LIBERTY
Great Marlborough Street
London W1B 5AH
Tel: 020 7734 1234
www.libertylondon.com
This famous London store
has always had a superb
sewing department and their
Liberty Lawn fabrics are
never out of fashion. Also has
an online shop.

MACCULLOCH & WALLIS
25–26 Poland Street
London W1F 8QN
Tel: 020 7629 0311
www.macculloch-wallis.co.uk
The ultimate, old-school
haberdashery and fabric
store in Central London, plus
an online shop. Frankly, they
have it all.

QUAY ANTIQUES CENTRE
Topsham
Exeter
Devon
Tel: 01392 874006
www.quayantiques.com
A treasure trove of vintage
table decorations, buttons,
and homeware.

VV ROULEAUX
102 Marylebone Lane
London W1U 2QD
Tel: 020 7224 5179
www.vvrouleaux.com
An inspirational source of
ribbons and all kinds of
trimmings to give your
projects that all-important
finishing touch.

SEW ESSENTIAL
Unit 4 Marquis Court
Marquis Drive
Moira
Swadlincote DE12 6E5
Tel: 01283 210422
www.sewessential.co.uk
Online sewing supplies with
a massive product range.
They are based in
Swadlincote and ship
worldwide.

SEW AND SEW
23 Canford Lane
Bristol BS9 3DQ
Tel: 0117 950 4995
Notions (haberdashery) for
sewing, knitting, crochet,
jewelry making, and crafts.

US

BRITEX FABRICS
117 Post Street
San Francisco
CA 94108
Tel: 415-392-2910
www.britexfabrics.com
Wide range of fabrics and
notions.

FABRIC DEPOT
10490 Baur Blvd
St. Louis
MO 63132
Tel: 800-468-0602
www.fabricdepot.com
Fabric and sewing supplies;
they have a store in St. Louis
and an online store.

FABRICLAND
270 US-22 West
Green Brook
NJ 08812
Tel: 908-755-4700
www.fabricland.com
Fabric and sewing supplies;
they also run fun events and
sewing classes.

HOBBY LOBBY
www.hobbylobby.com
Craft and hobby supplies;
stores nationwide.

JOANN FABRIC & CRAFT STORES
www.joann.com
Craft and hobby supplies;
stores nationwide.

MOOD DESIGNER FABRICS
Tel: 855-630-6663
www.moodfabrics.com
Fabric and sewing supplies;
they have two stores, in New
York and Los Angeles, as
well as an online store.

MICHAELS
Tel: 800-642-4235
www.michaels.com
Craft and hobby supplies,
including beads and buttons;
stores nationwide.

PURL SOHO
459 Broome Street
New York NY 10013
Tel: 212-420-8796
www.purlsoho.com
Great range of fabrics,
notions, and craft tools.

INDEX

Bold pagination indicates techniques

ACKNOWLEDGMENTS

Thanks to Steve for all those late nights and for supporting me without question. I love you.

To Coleford for not having such long walks during the making of this book. I will make up for them now!

Thank you to all at CICO Books for your hard work and for being so enjoyable to work with. Special thanks to Cindy Richards for finding and believing in me and for your love of clothes! To Carmel Edmonds for her quick responses and gentle encouragement, to Sarah Hoggett for such patience and attention to detail, to Sally Powell for her artistic expertise, to Valentina for her design skills, to project photographers Emma Mitchell and Chris Bracewell, to stylists Rob Merrett and Jemima Bradley, and to Stephen Dew for his amazing artwork. Thank you, guys, for sharing the same vision as me!

Thank you to some of my friends who have helped me during the making of this book: Fran De'Ath, Annelies Puddy, Jenny Reeves, Katie Brokinshire, Marguerite Fry, Edith Duvivier-Stuart, Jenni Joule, and Rebekah Johnston Smith. You are all amazingly talented—don't ever stop!

To Diana, Sylvia, and David for being such a source of inspiration from such a young age. Your taste in vintage is divine and I wouldn't have followed this path if it hadn't been for you. To Eileen Hilda Chisholm for her designer talents and to Edith Hayward for her tailoring skills and sewing machine.

To Davina Louise Lund for loving all things girly and for being someone who I can happily witter the hours away with talking about our love of clothes!

To all the girls: you know who I mean! You are a source of strength and inspiration. Thank you for helping me learn about you all through our seasonal fashion shows!

Thank you to the girls at Sew and Sew for being so helpful, patient, and supportive!

To David Pyne from the Tobacco Factory Market and to Helen Huertas from St Nicholas Market; you are both amazing and your vision for markets is spot on.

Last but definitely not least, thanks to my savvy publicist, Sarah Baker, who has championed me so well, and to Ali Cook from Bristol Vintage who introduced us.